GERARD DEPARDIEU ON SCREEN

By Chris Wade

Gerard Depardieu: On Screen
by Chris Wade

Wisdom Twins Books, 2020
wisdomtwinsbooks.weebly.com

Text Copyright of Chris Wade, 2020

Gerard Depardieu
On Screen

CONTENTS

INTRODUCTION

"I am the perfect turncoat," Gerard Depardieu once said, alluding to his versatility as a screen actor. Though he'd never say so himself, Gerard has an ability to hop effortlessly and gracefully from one genre to another, juggling film parts so different from the last that it seems impossible that one man could pull off such a smooth and seamless transformation. He is a chameleon, yet one who always remains very much the Gerard Depardieu we all know.

Emerging in the 1970s in the work of, among others, Bertrand Blier and Marguerite Duras, Depardieu was French cinema's wild man, dubbed the European De Niro, a figure of unpredictable danger, and a man who combined sensitivity with menace, light humour with a genuinely intimidating air. His almost animal-like physicality made him appear brutish and crude, whereas his humanity, so clearly present on his unique and highly watchable face, gave him a depth few others had.

He was, and still is, the ultimate screen actor, that of a rare breed who have their own style, can remain themselves in any film but at the same time make each part totally unique. Like Marcello Mastroianni, even Jack Nicholson, he is naturally charismatic, and lifts any script he is given, good or bad, into a wholly different realm. He is, in short, one of the finest actors the cinema has ever seen.

"I got into acting to try not to be taken for what I looked like - a hoodlum," he once told the New York Times. "Acting saved me. Otherwise, I would have become a killer." Though a dramatic statement perfect for the media, a sound byte if there ever was one, one suspects Depardieu's words are not a huge exaggeration. Indeed, he had a colourful past, running away from home at 12, living rough and then hooking up with prostitutes who tattooed and cared for him. He worked as a beach boy in the summer, but before this he'd made his money with petty crime. But it all suddenly turned around for Gerard, and he found he had an aim in life, a new direction. One day when a friend was auditioning for an acting role, Gerard went along too and fell into the business, starting with stage work before transitioning to the screen. If he hadn't chanced upon acting, lord knows where he might have ended up. These are the myths of Depardieu folk lore, and they can be exaggerated from time to time. But in general, there is some truth in the fact that without acting, Depardieu might have drifted into more serious crime.

He first came to prominence in Bertrand Blier's surreal tales, like Going Places (1974), Get Out Your Handkerchiefs (1978) and Buffet Froid (1979), while also working for Bernardo Bertolluci on 1900 (released in 1976), Marco Ferreri on The Last Woman (1976), and among others, Francois Truffaut on The Last Metro and The Woman Next Door (1980 and 81). Depardieu also made advances for director Maurice Pialat in his cult classic, Loulou (1980). Here, in a few short years, he established himself as cinema's edgiest young thespian, a man who dove into roles without too much thought and pontification, who worked on feeling and truth, not technique and dissection. He seemed to jump light years still as the 1980s went on, being staggeringly good in a run of classics, like The Return of Martin Guerre (1982), Jean de Florette (1986) and, for Pialat again, Under the Sun of Satan (1987). Listing all the classics he made in France through the 70s to the 90s is embarrassing for any other actor claiming to be France's leading performer, but Depardieu has never been pretentious or arrogant about his iconic status. If anything, he is self depreciating, characterising himself as a hooligan, a working class thug who got lucky and in the mean time, while enjoying success, taught himself and learned about the world in the process. But the fact is, few actors could hope to match him, especially when he was in his prime.

And "prime" is a funny word, for though some cruelly choose to highlight his infamous excesses and weight gain as signs of some great decline into mediocrity as a self lampooning caricature, the truth is he continues to give tremendous performances, while his age and extra pounds often only add magnitude and poignancy to his work. Yet even with recent works like Welcome to New York, Mammuth and Valley of Love, Depardieu remains a cartoonish figure to some, a fallen idol more interested in boozing and rubbing shoulders with Putin than making good films.

Sadly - and this being something Depardieu himself has noticed - his off camera antics often get more attention than any of the many wonderful performances ever do. A man once adored across the world for his work, recognised as the finest French actor of all time, famous for Cyrano de Bergerac and tons of masterpieces, is now more known as tabloid fodder, the man who supposedly put down France and chose Russia as his new adoptive home. Indeed, the character of Depardieu, the bloated, heavy drinking "buffoon" as many undeservedly view him, the man who fell off his scooter and often appeared on the cover of

Charlie Hebdo as a cartoon drunk, is now more known than the actor. "When I travel around the world what people know is that I pissed on a plane, that I'm Russian and that I wrote a letter of complaint to the prime minister," Depardieu recently observed with a slight hint of dissatisfaction, though he is not one to care too much about other people's perceptions of him. He lives life, devours it in fact, and his life style and career choices reflect this. He is out for new experiences, on and off camera, the film work an extension of his real life adventures.

Anyone who wants a glimpse into Depardieu the man, his views on France, Russia, politics, class and life in general, should read his essential book, Innocent, where he muses on all these subjects and many more. More interesting than his private life though, for me at least, is the body of work. While I would find it impossible to review all his films in one book, I did want to explore as many of his key credits as possible, and I do feel this volume gives the reader a decent summary of his career on screen. By looking at his most powerful and important performances, so is revealed his staggering range as an actor. There is a lot of ground covered here and if a newcomer to Gerard's filmography were to explore these titles in chronological order they would have a good idea why Depardieu was, and to some still is, so revered. Covering stand out films and roles from his earliest years (Nathalie Granger, Going Places, 1900, Maitresse), through the height of his fame (Martin Guerre, Jean de Florette, Under the Sun of Satan, Cyrano de Bergerac, Green Card) and to more recent works (Mammuth, Valley of Love, Marseille), one gets a sense of the sheer size of Depardieu's contribution to world cinema and the overwhelming volume of acting tour de forces. I also look into lesser known films, like 1988's sadly obscure A Strange Place to Meet with Catherine Deneuve, alongside classics like his TV version of The Count of Monte Cristo, 1985's Police, Blier's Palme d'Or winning Too Beautiful For You, and his memorable films with Isabelle Adjani, namely, as well as Mammuth, Barocco and Camille Claudel.

This is a hugely important and influential body of work, and it should not be overlooked, no matter how many headline grabbing antics the great man gets up to off screen. These films deserve to be remembered and celebrated. So whether you're an experienced Depardieu fan, or largely unfamiliar with his filmography, I hope this book is helpful and enjoyable.

THE FILMS

NATHALIE GRANGER (1972)

Marguerite Duras was one of France's leading writers, penning influential novels such as L'Ament (1984). Her huge bibliography aside, Duras also left behind a body of work in the cinema, not just as screenwriter, but also as director. Her films were highly individualistic, minimalist in style and presentation, and a million miles away from the popular idea of cinema as a narrative story. An acquired taste, they remain fascinating viewing.

Her 1972 film Nathalie Granger is perhaps her most well known work as a director, a haunting and strangely soothing experience which stays long in the mind after viewing and, despite not being the most activity-packed film, is still one which requires repeated viewings. Compulsive and addictive, it's both unsettling and inviting, a paradoxical non-story which for some will be like watching paint dry, but for others will be a completely unique hour and twenty minutes.

It stars Lucia Bose (a recent victim of COVID, who was sadly killed by the virus this year) as Isabelle, a woman living with another lady whose name we never learn, played by the wonderful and hypnotic Jeanne Moreau. Seemingly living together, we follow them throughout a largely non eventful day, pottering around their often ghostly home as they listen to radio broadcasts concerning a gang of teenage killers and the disappearance of a girl named Nathalie, clearly the daughter of Isabelle, who seems to have been far from your average girl. As the day goes on, the two women continue to exist in a strange, almost zombified state, as if waiting for something to happen (which never does, I might add). They perform everyday rituals, clean the table in a meditatively slow and intoxicating manner, and at one point, in a bit of subtle humour, Moreau answers a ringing phone, hilariously telling the caller they must have the wrong number because "there is no phone here."

Mid way through the film, Gerard Depardieu, in his first film role of genuine note, appears as a washing machine salesman. Trying to sell such an item to these two women though, proves a formidable task, and faced by their intimidating disinterest, he not only fails to make them see the wonders of this wonderful new machine, he is also convinced that he isn't much of a salesman and that this really isn't the job for him.

Shot in beautiful crisp black and white, Nathalie Granger is indeed a treat on the eyes, ensuring that even empty rooms, plain walls, tidy tables and sparse gardens are captivating. Of course, the elevation of the mundane and inanimate is down to the inactivity, Duras inviting us to fill in our own gaps, enjoy the silences and appreciate the voids for the truth they are. This is a greatly mysterious portrait of two women knowing something we don't, never informing we the viewer of what it is, though we suspect something sinister. Nathalie herself becomes an elusive enigma, rarely seen but always felt, reminded of in notes left behind and ghostly glimpses, sounds of her playing away like a normal child, only one who harbours something else unexplainable, indefinable.

Moreau and Bose are totally compelling in their roles, though they are not performances as such, but weirdly life-like acts of simply being. They inhabit their surroundings with silence, a combination of unease and comfort, though they are more often than not unnerving to watch, even if the film itself as a calming transcendent feel beneath the vague air of menace. Duras chose her leads well and she could not have found two more watchable, striking women, Moreau in particular who, as ever, is a pleasure to study, her every movement and gesture saying so much more than a paragraph of dialogue ever could. Lest we forget, Moreau had already acted for Michelangelo Antonioni at this point, embodying modern feminine disillusionment in his seminal 1961 work, La notte. Though Moreau was open with the fact she did not enjoy working with Antonioni, the results were rewarding in that they proved Moreau could summarise a whole vibe, perhaps a whole generation of women, expected to exist in the shadow of the male but wanting so much more out of life. She has a similar existentialist attitude here, mostly silent but saying a lot in her presence alone. In her earthy beauty and subtle sexuality, she is utterly captivating.

The film, as I mentioned, has only slight dashes of humour, and it is Depardieu who provides the film with its one fully comic scene, though the humour comes out of total discomfort, what modern viewers might call the cringe factor. His first scene, waxing lyrical on the washing machine to utter silence and deadly stares from two women who look as if they might eat him alive, is a masterclass in acting from all three parties, Depardieu laughing nervously, fidgeting, eventually cracking all together when he realises he really isn't much of a salesman. This scene in itself could have been an independent short film, but it works wonderfully within Duras' framework of the complete picture, providing weird relief from the stony silences and radio speech.

One could say that Duras discovered Depardieu and brought him to the attention of the serious movie-goer in this film. He may be inept nervousness personified in the failed hard-sell scene, but when he returns later on, prowling the corridors and then hanging round the kitchen blank faced, he takes on an airy, empty feel, becoming Duras' disconnected male, to whom women are aliens and life itself is a complete puzzle impossible to solve.

In a 2009 interview, Gerard spoke about first meeting Duras, the woman who had such a lasting effect on his life and film career: "I arrive at her home in the rue Saint-Benoît, she opens the door for me, slips off to the end of the corridor, looking even smaller. Walk toward me…, she whispered, walk toward me…. I was fresh from my small town, I said to myself, They're bizarre, these Parisians, but OK… And when I was literally on top of her, suffocating her, at the end of the corridor, Marguerite pressed her little head on my chest and, catching her breath, murmured: Stop, you're scaring me! That's good!"

"I had never seen anything like him" said Duras. "Natural genius, incredible intelligence and completely unspoiled. He didn't dare talk in those days. I'm not sure he knew how to read and write. During the filming, Jeanne Moreau said, 'I wonder where Marguerite found a Shakespearean actor?' She felt that dimension right away."

One can understand why Duras cast him; here he has two elements fully formed which ensured stardom and acclaim came quickly to Depardieu's door, the winning combination of menace, at least in his physicality, and insecure sensitivity. Both traits work off each other, so we warm to him but are also aware of his potential danger. Though he would explore this more, if unconsciously, in future films, Nathalie Granger is in some ways the essential starting point for Depardieu the quintessential French screen star. He arrived formed in Nathalie Granger, a star in the making able to hold his own amidst two of the finest European actresses of the era.

For those familiar with Duras' work and French cinema of the sixties and seventies, Nathalie Granger is a standout, though it is far more obscure these days than it deserves to be. Admirers of Depardieu and his more acclaimed performances will find his work here fascinating, a man usually so explosive and untameable (one might say he is often feral) keeping on the lid in the most curious, insidious yet stripped back film imaginable. A rare treat.

GOING PLACES (1974)

The film which signalled the true arrival on our screens of Gerard Depardieu was Bertrand Blier's outrageous black comedy, Going Places, titled Les Valseuses in French and based on Blier's own novel. Here, the twenty five year old actor, still fresh faced and dangerous, starred as Jean-Claude, who with his friend Pierrot (Patrick Dewaere) embarks on a road trip around France. The two young men are petty criminals and spend their time hustling, stealing, taking what they want and engaging in the most sordid of activities.

Going Places begins with the terrible duo stealing the car of a hairdresser, who pulls a gun on them when they return his vehicle (their defence is that they merely borrowed his car and always intended to bring it back). When they snatch the weapon, they take his assistant Marie-Ange (Miou-Miou) as a prisoner. While acting as her captors, they both have sex with her, but grow frustrated with the fact she cannot achieve an orgasm. Quickly dumping her off, they grow tired of frigid young ladies (lumps of meat as Jean-Claude refers to them) and opt to find a more mature woman who will be in control of her body, but also grateful for the attention of two young men.

They wait outside a prison, where Jeanne (the wonderful Jeanne Moreau) is just being released. Following her down the road, they latch on to her and quiz her about her life. Learning she has no money and nowhere to go, the boys hand over some of their stolen cash and wait outside a department store while Jeanne buys some new clothes. They take her to a cafe and enjoy a lavish meal, before deciding to get a hotel room and have a threesome. The next morning, while the young men sleep, Jeanne goes into the spare bedroom in the hotel, takes out the gun, and shoots herself, not in the head, but up her own vagina. Horrified, the boys get dressed and rush out of the hotel through the basement.

Researching the letters in the dead woman's case, they learn of her imprisoned son and the fact he too is about to be released. Picking him up, they take Jacques to their country retreat, where Marie-Ange is now set up as their female accomplice/casual sex partner. There is a new obsession with ensuring she achieves a climax, which Jacques, not Jean-Claude or Pierrot, manages to help her reach. While they toy with the idea of being a crime committing foursome, this plan crumbles apart. The final ten minutes involve the two boys and Marie-Ange coming across a family enjoying a picnic by a river, and plucking the daughter (played by a young Isabelle Huppert) away from the family unit in order to ceremoniously de-flower her. The film ends with the trio, after dropping off the young girl having taken her virginity, driving off in their latest stolen car, entering a long dark tunnel, going places but really heading nowhere.

Blier's film is a wonderful black comedy, raising genuine laughs which are inevitably tinged with guilt once you realise what you are actually laughing at. Both uncomfortably confrontational and genuinely hilarious, Blier succeeds because one is not asked to judge or celebrate the young men's shenanigans. Yes what they are doing is wrong, but the film is not weighed down by judgements, nor encumbered by a conscience. We follow the men in their aimless journey, not because we like them (indeed, they are two of the most loathsome louts ever shown on screen), but because we are desperate to know what's coming next. Their adventures do not seem contrived and the humour is never forced; it's very natural indeed, and played with the kind of genuine straight forwardness which makes it truly funny rather than merely amusing in a broad, caricature-like sense.

Blier's direction is assured and unfussy, while his script (co-written with Philippe Cumarcay) is often genuinely shocking and to some will be offensively misogynistic. That said, Pierrot and Jean-Claude are not gentlemen, and their harsh, often grotesque way with words fits the story perfectly. Yet had the film not starred Depardieu and Dewaere as the two restless crooks, Going Places may have been unwatchable. Depardieu in particular is brilliant, looking like he has genuinely just walked from the streets where he might have been swindling some poor unsuspecting person. Had we been told he had just stolen a car to drive to the shooting location, we would not have been surprised. No performance this good could possibly have gone unnoticed and it's perfectly logical that he became an overnight star after the film's smash success in France (it was the third most successful film that year). Alive, often frightening and seemingly always on the cusp of doing something either disgusting or totally unexpected, Depardieu's Jean-Claude is one of his finest cinematic creations. It seems though that the danger so evident in the performance was not entirely brought out of thin air. According to reports, Depardieu was still very much the wild man of his youth while making Going Places. Blier recalled that they often had to keep checking on him, as he had a habit of going off into the rougher areas of where they were shooting to pick fights in bars.

Going Places caused quite a stir upon release, being both commercially successful and extremely controversial, due to the dialogue, the lurid content, casual, blatant sex scenes and general carelessness of the characters. It was hedonism at his wildest, and seems to have divided audiences and critics alike. Roger Ebert, though seeing some worth in it, seems to have been sickened overall: "Despite its occasional charm, its several amusing moments and the touching scenes played by Jeanne Moreau, Going Places is a film of truly cynical decadence. It's also, not incidentally, the most misogynistic movie I can remember; its hatred of women is palpable and embarrassing. I came away from Going Places feeling that I'd spent two hours in the company of a filmmaker I would never want to meet."

Such critics seemed to miss the point. Blier himself was not the sexist one, he was just a man presenting certain views held by a particular type of young male. The fact he made us laugh and gasp at such men though, is an achievement indeed, and it's this mix of reactions which makes Going Places truly unique. Blier went on to further success in his career as a filmmaker, winning an Oscar for his 1977 classic Get Your Handkerchiefs Out (again, with Gerard Depardieu), making seminal films like Buffet Froid and Merci La Vie, not to mention the Cesar and Cannes Special Prize winning Too Beautiful For You, but there is a vitality, energy and genuine danger in Going Places that makes it, quite possibly, his most lasting and enthralling work.

MAITRESSE (1976)

Many of Gerard Depardieu's early films were controversial, and the actor was certainly not afraid of taking on risqué subjects, but Barbet Schroeder's Maitresse was perhaps the most provocative from his earliest years. Still one to make certain people wince today, it is a bold and unflinching exploration of sadomasochism, with a story which lures you in from the opening scene and never lets go until its bizarre, but ultimately fitting, finale.

In this confrontational character study, Depardieu is cast as a small time crook named Olivier, one of the dangerous young males which he perfected in the formative days of his film stardom. Meeting up with an old friend after arriving in Paris, he helps him out in his job as a door to door salesman of fine art books. One day they knock on the door of an apartment, to be faced with Ariane (played by Bulle Ogier), who, half undressed, tells them her bath is flooding and that she will buy the whole bibliography if they get the tap to stop. After doing so, she casually remarks that the woman in the flat downstairs is away on holiday. With their interests piqued by this fact, Olivier and his chum return at night to break into the empty apartment, where they come across a whole plethora of S and M gear, not to mention a man, naked bound and gagged, in a cage. They then learn the flat belongs to Ariane, the girl from upstairs, which she uses as a base in which to see her clients. A dominatrix, she earns her money torturing men and women while helping them live out their strange, perverted sexual fantasies.

Olivier ends up in bed with Ariane that night, and in the morning, after a civilised breakfast, they head out together to the country, where they attend a sadomasochistic party at a manor belonging to Ariane. As the pair get closer, Olivier begins to help her in her work. Falling slowly in love, Ariane faces an inner conflict. She does not wish to fall in love; she has, after all, chosen her path, and there is no room for love. He on the other hand, has quickly become devoted to her and struggles with the lurid antics she performs for money. When he discovers that the much-spoken-of Gautier is her pimp, Olivier pays him a visit and insists he release her from his employment. Olivier, naively perhaps, suggests he will now see to her business. There is a twist however, and as Olivier has clearly overstepped a mark, he alienates Ariane. But can the pair, drawn so naturally together, be kept apart?

Schroeder had already directed three films before this, but Maitresse was his first to cause a real stir. Undoubtedly graphic for the time, it was obvious that the sexual scenes were going to be controversial. Upon its release, France had recently loosened up their rules regarding explicit imagery, and Maitresse clearly benefited from this era of liberal mindedness. It was overseas however where Maitresse experienced trouble. When the film was submitted to the BBFC in the UK, it was not given a certificate. "The actual scenes of fetishism," they wrote, "are miles in excess of anything we have ever passed in this field." Though the picture could not be legally shown in public cinemas, it was screened in various clubs and later given an X certificate in the early 1980s, but only once Schroeder agreed to cut the admittedly grotesque scene of a man's penis being nailed to a board. Only now is it available totally uncut as the director intended.

Naturally when anyone discusses the film it is the graphic material they tend to hone straight in on. In my view though, the sexual scenes are possibly the least interesting ones in the film. Indeed, it is the dynamic between Ariane and Olivier that is the most fascinating theme. She, a naturally dominant figure, automatically assumes an authoritarian role in her relationship with Olivier. As he is a penniless crook, she is the bread winner, and it is she who hands money over to him, making him a more traditional stay at home sort. However, given Depardieu's more brutish manner and formidable physical presence, the relationship is not so straight forward. Despite her dominant character, he is clearly the man, more dominant sexually, and he is far from being anything like one of her submissive customers, who invite punishment but shun traditional satisfaction. Naturally, there are complications in their life together, him jealous of the attention and care she bestows on the men who pay her for her services, she torn between a new love and the fact this man is invading on her independent life style.

Depardieu and Ogier both give believable, sincere performances; Ogier's Ariane is a contradictory figure who is merciless, soulless even, when performing her acts (though it's a put-on front to please her client, as she clearly enjoys her work), but a tender lover to Olivier and often light in humour and tone when the leather gear is in the wardrobe. Ariane is a professional and prides herself on ensuring her work is well played out and that her customers leave satisfied. But she can turn it off, only displaying masochistic tendencies outside the torture chamber in the smallest ways, such as when feeding insects to her Venus fly trap. Her sex with Olivier for instance, appears to be straight forward and, for want of a better word, normal.

Ogier had acted for Schroeder before in his previous film, La Vallee, but one could say this is perhaps the finest work she committed to celluloid. A charismatic and striking figure, it was clear that Schroeder, and the film itself, needed an actor capable of matching her. Ogier is so watchable, such a magnet for the attention of the viewer that a lesser actor, facing the task of facing up to her, may not have been up for the job. Schroeder chose Depardieu as Olivier, at that time one of the most exciting young actors in the world. He is, of course, excellent, effortlessly balancing the required rough-around-the-edges quality of a crook and the brittle sensitivity of a jealous lover. He goes from tough street fighter to naive, wide eyed man in love from scene to scene, but the mood changes never jar or seem heavy handed; Depardieu applies them with subtlety and authenticity.

Though the masochistic scenes are often very powerful, daring and wonderfully shot, it is due to the way Schroeder plays with gender stereotypes and taboos in the field of sexuality that Maitresse reaches another level. Thought provoking and genuinely surprising, at times going into totally unexpected territory, beneath the surface it's a straight forward love story, with the two lovers facing challenges which, though perverse, seem as believable as any of the more acceptable clichés getting in the way of your standard movie romance. As Maitresse is not sensationalised, and does not include the sadomasochistic scenes for the sake of sheer titillation (they are more disturbing than arousing), one becomes totally engaged with the fate of Olivier and Ariane's relationship. If anything, one gets so accustomed to the torture scenes that they seem no different to the idea of Ariane clocking in at an office everyday.

Schroeder himself gave a fascinating interview at a 2012 BFI screening of the movie, stating that they had to be very careful not to let the film be dominated (no pun intended) by the S and M scenes. He also wished to show the potential dangers of the job, and the sheer pressure Ariane is under in bringing to life these lurid fantasies. Perhaps most interesting of all is the fact that Schroeder originally wanted Olivier to begin exploring his own fantasies through Ariane's work, but decided to go with a more "classical progression... he wants to destroy the world he sees as his rival for Ariane's love." In the end, Depardieu's heavy handed, almost child-like Olivier was destined to be a jealous, possessive male.

There is one scene however which remains controversial, and that is the abattoir sequence, where we see the real killing of a horse, slaughtered to be cut up for horse meat. According to Schroeder the idea of the scene came from Depardieu, who told the director he often went to buy fresh horse meat from a butcher's at dawn. Schroeder included it at a vital moment, right after Olivier visits Gautier. Viewing the slaying of the poor creature was an act of self punishment, knowing he had gone too far by visiting Ariane's pimp. Still, it is much more disturbing than any of the S and M scenes, yet seems to get little attention these days.

It may have taken a while for Maitresse to be more widely appreciated, but now it's rightfully regarded as a European landmark. Time Out have called it "a wickedly funny fable on the more demanding side of love," while in 2016 the BBC's Mark Kermode picked it out as a film of the week on the BFI player.

Modern viewers, now more attuned to film violence and graphic sex, may wonder what all the fuss was about (indeed, many reviewers online have expressed this thought), but if underwhelmed by a film whose reputation precedes it, one hopes they will appreciate the unfolding plot and the two fine performances leading it into fascinating areas. Decades on, Maitresse is an essential part of 1970s French cinema, a film which remains powerful, provocative and both visually and intellectually engaging.

As an added note, Depardieu makes a mention of Maitresse in his fascinating book, Innocent. While discussing America's hypocrisy, on the surface a prudent country of good morals, he thought it hid its perversions in a dishonest manner. "When I did Maitresse it became a cult film in America. They watched it in secret."

1900 (1976)

1900 (1976)

1900 is a sprawling epic by Italian director Bernardo Bertolucci, an explicit but ultimately powerful telling of Italian life in the first half of the 20th Century. It follows two life long friends, Alfredo (De Niro) and Olmo (Gerard Depardieu), through World War 1, marriage, tragedy, and the arrival of the Second World War, ultimately separated by their very different political beliefs and backgrounds.

From the word go, 1900 is a heavily politicised piece, obviously very personal to Bertolucci. Rather crudely and unflinchingly, it hammers home the point of how the landowners allowed the rise of fascism. It is definitely left wing, and considering its butchering by the American film industry, was maybe just a bit too communistic for Hollywood. "Too many red flags," noted Bertolucci himself. But beneath the political statements, the film has some very memorable sequences, some of which are plain disturbing, and a story through its centre - that of two friends, divided by their class - which engages from start to finish. Certainly a difficult film to enjoy, it's a startling piece of work all the same.

The original director's cut of the film, now available on DVD, is 5 hours long and is certainly the definitive version to watch. Although long, it gives more detail, scope, horror and beauty to the story, being truer to Bertolucci's grand vision. The wider released version was just over 3 hours, therefore cutting off a whole 2 hours of interesting scenes, an act which must surely have devastated Bertolucci. There are other cuts and edits too; indeed, it has to be one of the most re-edited and re-cut films in Italian film history.

"When I finished the movie I said I couldn't cut one frame," Bertolucci said in a 1977 interview. "But later I saw that the movie could be cut. Instead of a castration, I arrived at an artistic work. What we have now is the film I want. I didn't remove any sequences. I cut short pieces of film. The difference is only in the rhythm. The meaning, the strength, is absolutely the same."

The actual shooting of 1900 was not without its complications and has gone down in film legend. Endlessly rewritten, with cast members storming off set and the budget spiralling way out of control, it's a miracle it got made at all. The superb cast, which Bertolucci hoped would give his film a credible commercial boost for world wide audiences, included Donald Sutherland as the evil Attila, plus Burt Lancaster and Sterling Hayden as the two grandfathers. Bertolucci's best casting decision was to pair up two of the world's most exciting young rising actors, Depardieu and De Niro, who are both on excellent form here, at a time when they were perhaps still hungry for success and recognition. One scene, now infamous, involves the two actors getting hand relief from the same woman (Stefani Casini) in a bed, all three of them totally naked. In fact the whole film is highly sexed, with flaccid and erect penises, bare breasts and scenes of almost depraved sexual desire littered throughout. Look past this though and there is a clarity to Bertolucci's message.

When casting the film, Bertolucci paid a visit to the US and saw some films at the cinema. One movie he saw was Mean Streets. Impressed by the lead actors, he knew he wanted one of them to play Alfredo. Floating between Harvey Keitel and De Niro, the director finally settled on asking De Niro, saying he seemed more working class. "I saw great mystery in him," he added.

De Niro plays an over privileged man born into money and although he may not be as outright awful as, say, his character Noodles in Once Upon A Time In America, Alfredo is certainly one of his least likeable creations. He is spoilt, ungrateful, irresponsible, weak, and virtually unable to stand up to, or indeed for, anything at all. On his role, De Niro later admitted that "Alfredo was an observer, it was difficult to fill him in." The main problem with his character is that he *has* no real character. He is the eyes of the film, and as De Niro himself said, merely an observer. Seeing as De Niro was in his acting prime around this time, it seems like a crime to not have used his power. He is at his best as a man of reaction, not as a push over. "Bertolucci has locked De Niro out as an actor," critic Pauline Kael observed. "Gutted him. His Alfedo is an unfinished man." She even went as far as to say that the Alfredo character was in fact the "bourgeois liberal" Bertolucci feared himself to be. Yes, the daggers were out for Bertolucci.

Crashing turbulently against De Niro is a brutishly good Depardieu, recently a new star of French cinema who was now seeing appreciation of his work spread across Europe and beyond. In his book Innocent, during a passage in which he waxes lyrical of the Russian people and explains his affinity with the land, he mentions that Bernardo hired him because, among other reasons, he wanted someone who looked Russian. He is the more arresting, urgent and straight forward of the two, a working class farm hand who is not afraid to get his hands dirty and is certainly more confrontational than his old friend. Whereas Alfredo speaks, Depardieu's character acts. He is also more feeling, more sensitive.

One of the main reasons to watch the film is to enjoy the brilliant performances from two actors who, though clearly different, were also rather similar in some ways. Physically there is a slight resemblance, but there is also an urgency and excitement about them which causes sparks of strange competitiveness. Indeed, watching Gerard and Robert at this early stage of their careers is a fulfilling experience. On set it appears that they got on well. Recently, Depardieu claims to have helped De Niro through the tricky sex scene, saying he made a concoction of Tiger Balm and water, which meant De Niro was able to stay erect for the full scene. It's a mere anecdote, but an amusing one all the same.

The film also features a marvellous turn from Sutherland as the vile Attila, and his sequences are some of the most horrific and unforgettable in the whole film. A complete bastard through and through, Sutherland is on electrifying form. And although the actor later claimed he couldn't bring himself to watch his turn in the film, as it genuinely upset him, it's still one of the most brutal and commanding performances of his whole career.

Bertolucci himself claimed he wanted the film to build a bridge between nations, but ultimately it failed in that respect. That said, 1900 is something to behold despite its viler moments. What it has going for it is the wonderful direction and another beautiful score from composer Ennio Morricone, in my book the best film composer of all time. But Bertolucci only served himself up for criticism with 1900 and reinforced his nickname as "the dirty old man of cinema." Still, it's a film well worth watching if you get the spare time.

A more recent interview with the man behind the film offered some insights into the genesis of 1900. "I wanted to make a kind of poem about where I was born, my family, the farmers, the land owners. This universe was very present in my childhood."

THE LAST WOMAN (1976)

While his name might not predominantly pop up when modern critics, especially those outside Italy, are discussing the maestros of Italian cinema, Marco Ferreri was one of the most outrageous, unique and brilliant filmmakers of his generation. Ferreri's films, often grotesque, often very funny and always compulsively watchable, are not easy to categorise today. Though he often found himself equally criticised and applauded, Ferreri was the kind of man who refused to bow down and make the kind of film expected of him. Most famous today for seminal classics like Dillinger is Dead (1969) and the hedonistic masterpiece La Grande Bouffe (1973), Ferreri's full oeuvre is one to behold, making it a shame indeed that some of his work is so hard to track down or remains unavailable commercially to a potential audience who would lap up his satirical, hard edged style of expressionism.

Characterising himself as both a feminist and a misogynist, many modern viewers may find Ferreri's work hopelessly un-PC, if not downright shocking. But if you can get past the fact they were made in a very different time, and were satirical, surrealistic and often symbolic of a greater picture, Ferreri's colourful, vibrant and fearless work will enlighten you.

In one interview he said: "I ask women to make for me a portrait of a woman and they always portray to me the Virgin Mary. So misogynist is not a word that makes sense. I think women are stronger than men. They represent the fantastic imagination side of men. I am always speaking as a European, not as an American."

"The Last Woman," he said in 1977, "is a political film. All my films are… the relationship between men and the world they live in." The film, a harsh, jagged and often unpleasant one, highlights the unrest and confusion between the male and the female, with Depardieu, as in Ferreri's later Bye Bye Monkey, playing a kind of primal male who loves his kin but struggles to see eye to eye with the women in his life. He is an engineer, who after his wife leaves him, wishing to spread her feminist wings, takes on custody of his infant son and also begins an affair with his day care worker, Valerie, played by the gorgeous Ornella Muti. Their passionate and very physical relationship fulfils his animalistic side, but when the mother comes back into the picture, the tryst threatens his chances of retaining custody. As the film goes on, Depardieu becomes increasingly frustrated and torn. The finale, most unexpected even for Ferreri, is one of the most outrageous final reels in film history.

This is a real stand out from Gerard's early years as a world renowned star, once again showing himself to be the bravest, most daring and least squeamish actor of his time. Still harbouring those street smarts, he is the raw male, symbolising the masculine caveman, quite often standing nude with chest stuck out, protecting the child he holds in one arm and holding his woman in the other, who he takes with passion whenever he pleases. This is the kind of Ferreri film they threw sexist and misogynist claims at, and though one can understand why it may be viewed negatively as pure sexism, Ferreri is merely reflecting a certain dissatisfaction amongst the more forceful, non-progressive, traditionalist males of the world. But for Ferreri, such claims were part of his job, and he expected a backlash seeing as he was exploring taboo ideas. He was damned a complete sexist when he made La Grande Bouffe, especially when he presented the four friends treating the hired women like the meat they gorged on in their orgy of decadence, but those critics were missing the point. As in Bye Bye Monkey, another Depardieu/Ferreri gem, he laments the downfall of the male and the uprising of the new modern woman. He is not saying this shift is right or wrong, he is simply commenting on it, another "political" film about the conflicts so inevitable between the opposing sexes.

Gerard is magnificent in this Cesar nominated effort, a man-child who will touch, fondle, feel and devour whatever he feels like. It is a primal, vital and quite often frighteningly intense performance, Depardieu the animal man turned up to eleven. In one sequence, unashamedly naked, he tries to attack a woman with a phallic object, a gigantic penis in fact, a moment which symbolises his anger and frustrations, that he merely wants to fuck and own, and fails to see where he fits into the feminist era.

The film was deemed too controversial for modern tastes and was banned in various countries. Even to this day, it's hard work tracking it down and it remains elusive, which is particularly frustrating for Ferreri completists and fans of Depardieu at his best. Thankfully though, finding The Last Woman is not impossible, but a bit of detective work might be in order. Easily offended viewers will, perhaps understandably, be put off by certain imagery in the film and Ferreri's cynical, often crude and occasionally heartless approach, but some valid and thought provoking themes are explored. The baby himself could be seen as a symbol for Depardieu's own sulky childishness, rather like the ape in Bye Bye Monkey symbolised his primal urges.

Many reviewers have found the film hard work. Time Out wrote "Here the boyish male sex object is Depardieu, but both he and the women in his life are painfully conscious that man cannot live by his cock alone. Depardieu, whose ideal is a life of eating, fucking and sleeping, is finally driven to self-mutilation in his inability to live up to his own patriarchal image of himself. It's as fraught and desperate as it sounds, and as laboriously worked out as you'd expect from the director of La Grande Bouffe; as there, though, the freshness of the performances just about makes the pessimism tolerable."

The Spanish publication El Pais, clearly seeing it as an experiment in social dynamics, made some interesting observations, writing in their review: "Not as clear as his previous films or as corrosive, Marco

Ferreri's recent chapter on the war between men and women works more as a cinematic exercise for students of sociology or psychoanalysis than for mere film aficionados."

The Last Woman is often a challenge, most certainly isn't for everyone, and occasionally leaves a bad taste in the mouth. But it is a very important Ferreri work, in a line of films which included Liza, La Grande Bouffe, Don't Touch the White Woman and Bye Bye Monkey. Though veering off now and then, and sometimes questionable with its upfront imagery, this unflinching film is essential Depardieu and a prime example of why he flew so quickly to world fame in the mid to late 1970s.

BAROCCO (1976)

Barocco is a raw, well paced and very gripping thriller from director Andre Techine, a film which potentially could have become just another pot boiler, a typical entry in its genre, but is in fact a very cleverly crafted, rather unexpected gem.

It stars Isabelle Adjani as Laure, a young woman who we first see visiting her boxer boyfriend Samson (Depardieu) in a gym where he is being photographed in the ring. Clearly washed up, he utters the immortal lines - to himself I might add - "how strange it would be to view this place through the eyes of a champion". It turns out that Samson is being offered a lot of money to give an interview stating he has had a gay affair with a well known politician, which he hasn't. Political competition is the motive, and though Samson doesn't like the idea, Laure pushes for it, tempted as she is by the huge sum of cash. When they are approached by the other side of the political race, they are offered the same sum to move away and shut their mouths on the ludicrous affair.

The plot takes a twist when Laure plans to meet Samson, but he is followed by two assassins and her plan to hide the money in a train locker goes awry. Laure waits for him all night in a diner and in the morning she is greeted by a man who is almost identical to Samson (played by Depardieu), who is in fact one of the assassins. When Samson arrives at the cafe, he is shot in the face and dies. From here the plot becomes more intense, Laure helping the police to catch the killer, who in turn has his eyes on the money.

Barocco is an exciting and enthralling ride from start to finish, driven by a truly excellent screenplay from Techine and Marilyn Goldin and a host of excellent performances. Depardieu is brilliant in the dual roles of the down on his luck, slightly over the hill boxer, a modest man as there has ever been, and the vicious dark haired killer, who is sinister and genuinely threatening. The best work here though, perhaps, comes from Adjani, in a tremendous display of exasperation and determination, an effort which holds the film together and ensures we the viewer are on board the whole way through.

Many have chosen to see Barocco as a fantasy rooted in cinematic history rather than as a straight forward thriller, which I personally prefer to enjoy it as. Yes there are homages to Hitchcock, Lang and others (the music even brings to mind the world of legendary composer Bernard Herrmann, in particular his score for Psycho), but Barocco is such a well played out thriller in its own right that seeing it as merely a homage does it a disservice. This said, it is not a realistic film at all, is certainly heightened, aware that it exists in the alternative world of film, and has an often dreamy, fantastical atmosphere. For instance, the murder of Samson in the snow is the sort of strangely beautiful moment that only happens in film (after all, is death ever beautiful in real life?), and the sight of his face, hazy and almost blurred through the window, is a purely cinematic image. Clearly, Therine wanted us to be aware of the differences between reality and film fantasy.

It received multiple nominations at the Cesar Awards, winning for its music, cinematography and a supporting turn by Marie-France Pisier, who is brilliant as Nelly, the prostitute friend who acts as a moral compass for Adjani's character. Depardieu and Adjani also deserved top honours, but didn't receive them. Barocco is widely available with English subtitles and is definitely essential for fans of early Depardieu.

LE CAMION (1977)

The combination of Gerard Depardieu and the great Marguerite Duras always produced films of the most unique atmosphere. They had first encountered one another in the early 1970s when Duras, now a legendary figure in literature an film, cast him as the crummy salesman in her 1972 masterpiece Nathalie Granger. Five years later, with Depardieu now established as a star and icon in his own right, he appeared alongside her in another enigmatic piece, Le Camion, often known as The Lorry and The Truck.

Written and directed by Duras, this reflective, strange, yet oddly soothing film features Marguerite herself, sat in a chair opposite a man known in the credits as simply "him". This is Depardieu playing an actor who is quietly listening to Duras explaining an outline of a script for her next movie. The "plot" of her film within a film (as much as you can call it that) concerns a female hitch-hiker who finds herself in a truck. While making her way across the country, she speaks to the driver who never utters a word in reply. Though we never see the driver nor the passenger, we hear their exchanges from the mouth of Duras, and the occasional quiet replies of Gerard.

If anyone were to chance upon The Truck in its opening reel, as the truck leaves the depot, heads for the road and makes way for Duras and Depardieu's names, then the title "Le Camion", one might be expecting to see a conventional movie, a road trip perhaps where Duras merely narrates the tale, her voice heard every now and then between the action (for want of a better word) and the dialogue between the two characters. A few minutes in however, faced with the sight of Duras and Depardieu, her protege in many ways, sitting comfortably in a dimly lit room, he with papers strewn about the place, listening intently, and it would become clear that this in itself is the picture. I personally had the advantage of already being aware of Duras' filmic style, having seen

Nathalie Granger, and knew all too well that Le Camion was going to at least be experimental. Though the concept itself may seem odd, boring to someone used to narrative cinema, it is a most meditative, beautiful and weirdly hypnotising piece, keeping you (or me at least) hooked, all the while knowing nothing remotely eventful is going to happen. It is in this state of knowing that La Camion becomes a somewhat addictive, gripping piece, despite ones' awareness of its direction.

Duras utters a line in the film which could be its tag: "The cinema stops the text and kills its offspring; the imagination". Duras is highlighting the paradoxical notion that as soon as a script makes it to filming, when the camera begins to roll, it is already dead, all potential hopes for its ultimate realisation gone. Once filming ends, it is finished, a piece that may or may not resemble the hopes of the original vision laid out mentally by the creator. By showing us the truck and the scenery as it passes by, Duras de-constructs, very quietly I might add, the concept of film, its whole purpose to combine interesting visuals with a plot. By limiting it to Duras and Depardieu in the darkness, and the beautifully shot sequences of the truck in motion, our own imaginations are given the space to run free. It is a proto-film, a fill-in-the-gaps experience where Duras offers the viewer a chance to envision the events. This said, the dialogue between the driver and the passenger is clear enough, that she is against communism and he finds her to be a reactionary, so at least in its words the film is realised.

Depardieu is a curious presence here, in between his massively prolific year in 1976 (where he made such films as The Last Woman, 1900, Maitresse and Barocco) and 1978, when he starred in Bertrand Blier's Get Out Your Handkerchiefs. There is none of the menace and rawness he exhibits in these more confrontational films, but a quiet, modest side, looking as if he is genuinely fascinated by Duras' words and the scenario he, like us, is picturing in his mind. He is her audience, her soundboard, occasionally asking questions but for the most part listening intently. They make for a compulsively watchable duo.

It divided viewers at the Cannes Film Festival but attracted its fair share of admiration, particularly from Pauline Kael, who reviewed it for the New Yorker the same week as she reviewed the release of the original Star Wars. While liking both, she devoted more time to Duras' The Truck. "In her new film," wrote Kael, "she has become a master. Duras doesn't even get near the mass of moviegoers, though somehow—God knows how—she manages to make her own pictures, her own way. Hers is possibly the most sadomasochistic of all director relationships with the audience: she drives people out of the theatre, while, no doubt, scorning them for their childish obtuseness. At the same time, she must be suffering from her lack of popularity. Her battle with the audience reaches a new stage in The Truck, in which the split between her artistry and what the public wants is pointed up and turned against the audience. She brings it off, but she's doing herself in, too. And so it isn't a simple prank."

Duras has a point in that the film feels like a mischievous prank, but to enjoy it one must separate it from ones' familiarity with and expectations of cinema (after all, we are all conditioned to appreciate the conventional mainstream movies) and place The Truck in another area all together. More of an experience (and a strange one at that) than a film, it is "art cinema" in the best possible way, an experiment in form and convention.

Kael also wrote, "Duras reads aloud the script of a film in which Depardieu would act the role of a truck driver who picks up a woman hitchhiker. He would drive and ask a question or two; the woman would talk. Depardieu doesn't actually play the truck driver: this actor, whose physical and emotional weight can fill up the screen, is used as a nonprofessional. He merely listens trustingly, a friend, a student, as Duras reads. Hers is the only performance, and there has never been anything like it: controlling the whole movie visibly, from her position on the screen as creator-star, she is so assured that there is no skittish need for makeup, no nerves, quick gestures, tics."

I am not going to suggest that this film is for everyone, or that every Depardieu admirer will enjoy it, but I do feel it's a vital entry in his filmography. It is a film he made for/with one of his mentors, an elder from whom he learned a great deal, and who left a lasting impression on him. Gerard could and would not make anyone a list of his most important films, but I do feel The Truck is an essential stop in that vast canon of his. There is another side of Depardieu here, the intent listener, the receptacle for Duras's wisdom. This is not of course a performance we are seeing from Depardieu (Duras is giving the performance of course), but another form of simply being, and it's hypnotically brilliant.

BYE BYE MONKEY (1978)

Marco Ferreri repeatedly pushed the boundaries in his films, but Bye Bye Monkey is among his most extreme, unsettling, thought provoking, utterly bonkers movies - and that is saying something. Though perhaps less focused and powerful than La Grande Bouffe (in my view his true masterpiece), Bye Bye Monkey is certainly wilder (if that were possible), weirder, and seems to be saying so much more about society as a whole, but especially modern America. It is also, of course, brilliant.

Gerard Depardieu stars as Lafayette, a New York based electrician who does work for a wax museum run by the very strange Andreas (James Coco), mostly focused on Ancient Imperial Rome, and a feminist theatre troupe who need him for their lighting tricks. There are other key figures in the film too; for instance, Marcello Mastroianni plays Luigi, an extremely eccentric immigrant who hangs around with other unusual characters near the beach, including Mrs Toland, played by Geraldine Fitzgerald. One day, the theatre troupe, who are playing with the idea of exploring rape in their dramatic work, realise they have no experience of it themselves, so decide to rape Lafayette. One girl, Angelica (Abigal Clayton), acts as the chief rapist and afterwards begins to date him. But things haven't even got started at this point. One day, Lafayaette, Luigi and other friends take a visit to the beach, where they find a gigantic sculpture of an ape (most literally a deceased King Kong; symbolically the bulky remains of manhood), lying in a heap on the sand. This image is striking enough of course, but to make it even more remarkable is the fact that an actual baby chimp emerges from its folds. Luigi picks it up, insisting it's his son, but the baby falls into the care of Lafayette when Luigi claims he's too old to be a dad.

The chimp then moves into Lafayette's seedy apartment, which is infested with rats. As the movie goes on, Lafayette and the chimp bond, having various adventures together as they make their way around the more run down parts of New York City. The atmosphere is unnerving for much of the film, but strangely there is true warmth between man and ape. However, in the final quarter or so, the movie becomes increasingly dark, unflinchingly so, and ends in the kind of tragedy the whole film seems to have been silently building towards, in what is one of the saddest and most horrifying climaxes to any picture I have ever seen.

Though Ferreri often stated in interviews that everything in his films should be enjoyed at face value, taken literally and not dissected for hidden meanings until all the fun has been intellectualised out of it, there is no doubting that he was being mischievous with such a statement, for his films are full of symbolism. The symbolism in La Grande Bouffe for instance was blatantly obvious and more effective than subtly applied allegories could ever be. In Bye Bye Monkey, with the narrative being anarchic, and with nothing out of reach of Ferreri's savage satire, it's harder to pin point what he precisely means in each scene. Some have seen Bye Bye Monkey as an anti feminist film - even an anti female film! After all, Lafayette chooses the ape over his girlfriend who is carrying his child, though in my view his bond with the ape merely reflects Lafayette's primal humanity, him being a man living in a world of crumbling values, drawn to the simplicity and purity of the creature. Indeed, clinging to the chimp ensures Lafayette soaks in some of that innocence. Even though one cannot deny that Ferreri paints the feminist troupe as dangerously angry and aggressive, they are in fact the only stable people in the whole film. For me, the feminist theories are misleading; clearly, with Ferreri depicting New York as some crumbling hellhole, the film laments the lack of humanity in modern society, with the ape as child, wide eyed and innocent in the face of corruption and decay. But one could validly say that this film, like some of his others, also laments the death of traditional manhood, that man himself was being robbed off his masculinity out of guilt and shame. (Mastroiani's Luigi seems to sum this up in one line, when sexually frustrated shouting out, "I have some kind of monster between my legs!") Though this arguably misogynistic view will automatically put off some viewers, it's best to keep an open mind. Again, it is not as simple as Ferreri mourning masculinity or indeed mankind itself, but perhaps the values of old. And just because his characters are tearful of the changing times, does not mean Ferreri or the younger characters are. This in mind, there is so much haunting and disturbing imagery here that it's impossible to rip away its vitality by trying to hang meanings on every frame. It's best in some ways to sit back and enjoy (or depending on your view, endure) the odd ball delights unfolding before your eyes.

Depardieu is brilliant in the lead role, this being another one of his macho, streetwise grafters. Depardieu is also convincing as a father, and the fact the child is an ape makes no real difference. He has an amused manner about him, and retains his sexist views despite being challenged by the feminists. Though Depardieu is our eyes throughout, Mastroianni's Luigi is in some ways the most engaging, mysterious and bizarre character in the film. An ageing Italian, he paints the figurines in the museum, solemnly I might add, always complaining that he cannot find love or sex in America because modern women don't respect their elders, or the old fashioned way a man once related to a woman. Always moist eyed, often with tears running down his cheeks, he is a raw man in torment; defeated, lost, always a "wop", an outsider, someone on the fringes, not just within society, but even amongst his fellow eccentrics. In one scene he does look briefly happy, when he begins an impromptu tap dance with his cane. When he drops it however, he instantly resumes his sombre state. Unfortunately he meets a tragic and extremely disturbing end, but it's also one of Marcello's most memorable exits.

As Andreas, James Coco is also fascinating, a man obsessed with the certainty of history, the grandness of Ancient Rome, who exists in his own world away from the modern day rot outside his bizarre museum. He recites dramatic speeches in the dark, standing amidst his wax creations as if he were one himself, and in one scene receives fellatio while educating the performer of the sexual act on the rich subject of Roman history. One of the most revealing parts is when his museum is judged to be unfit by a mysterious American figure from a psychological department of the government, who offers Andreas a bribe if he will slowly and subtly repaint his Roman heroes into American presidents. Ferreri is clearly attacking America's arrogant habit of rewriting history, of their cold hearted imperialism and insistence that they are always right. Morally and physically, judging by the vermin infested New York of Bye Bye Monkey, America is heading down the toilet where it belongs. Though as insane and erratic as everyone else in the film, Andreas's words at least make sense. He acts as a kind of demented tour guide, not just in the museum, but in the film itself, regularly punctuating the surreal symbolism and scenarios with dialogue that reminds everyone, himself included, that they are doomed.

Bye Bye Monkey won the main prize at Cannes, even though some critics were hopelessly lost amidst its surrealistic liberation. For those with an attention span longer than five minutes however, Bye Bye Monkey is a thought provoking, funny, often very bleak but ultimately enjoyable (if that is indeed the correct word) and hugely rewarding film of imagination, a movie with more ideas in five of its minutes than any modern blockbuster has in all its CGI stuffed scenes of nothingness. Its streets devoid of life, save the scurrying of rats and the odd eccentric, stick in the mind forever. Love it or hate it, you will never see another movie like Bye Bye Monkey.

GET OUT YOUR HANDKERCHIEFS (1978)

Bertrand Blier is one of the most unique and individual directors in cinema history. Truly surrealistic, his films dispense with all logic, but rather than dissolving in a form of Dada nonsense, they give birth to their own new logic in the process, presenting the viewer with so many unexpected, provocative twists and turns that after a while, thanks largely to the deadpan reactions of the actors, the viewer accepts them at face value. After ten minutes of any Blier film, nothing can be questioned; nor, for that matter, can it be answered.

Depardieu had become a star in Blier's wonderfully mad Going Places, and his next film with the director, some four years later with Gerard established firmly as a new bright light of world cinema, was the outrageously funny, and often plain shocking, Get Out Your Handkerchiefs. Undeniably subversive, it seems bizarre today that such a straight laced institution as the Oscars would give such a grimy, strange film its Best Foreign Language Film gong - which it did, in 1978. It's hard to imagine it doing so in today's social climate.

The film stars Depardieu as Raoul, a young driving instructor married to Solange (Carole Laure), and experiencing a certain dissatisfaction with their stale, increasingly strained relationship. Dining out one Sunday lunch time, Raoul becomes overwhelmed with frustration, and insists that his wife is sick of his face, and that she needs, in his words, "a new pair of eyes and balls". Driven to cheer up his wife, he goes to another table and meets Stephane (Patrick Dewaere), a teacher reading about Mozart, and offers him the opportunity to finish the meal with his wife and hopefully make her smile. As the film progresses, the three characters become a trio, each man taking it in turns to spend the night with Solange in a bid to liven her up. When both men come to the bizarre conclusion that Solange's passionless state (she never smiles or laughs, preferring to sit quietly knitting for hours on end) will be lifted by a pregnancy, they attempt to impregnate her. The neighbour also enters the situation, though he does not engage with Solange and merely joins in with the boys and their weird obsession with the life and work of Mozart, who they regularly lament.

The film takes a weird twist when Stephane takes a class of boys to a summer camp, and Solange and Raoul accompany him as unlikely assistant teachers. Unexpectedly, Solange falls for Christian (Riton Liebman), a 13 year old child genius who enchants her from the word go. Bullied by the other children, she takes pity on him, invites him into her bed and eventually, after a brief disagreement, opens him up to the wonders of femininity. When he expresses his reluctance to return to his family, he is sent to the boarding school, but the terrible trio kidnap him, as Solange can not go on living without her boy. As Raoul and Stephane become more jealous of the young boy, there comes forth a revelation which, even to the usual standards of Blier's work, is most unexpected, though not at all illogical given the way things have been heading. It is perhaps one of the best finales in the history of European cinema.

"I thought about the film on and off for about three years before I began writing," Blier said in 1979. "So when I did write, the ideas came out spontaneously. I almost didn't know what I was writing. What I like in films and in literature are stories and characters that surprise me."

Get Out Your Handkerchiefs certainly gives its viewer a lot to think about, but most of all it offers us much to react to, and after each viewing one is forced (or feels the need) to sit back and re-think what we've seen and experienced. Totally individualistic, it manages to tear everything out of the rule book, reshuffle it, batter it beyond recognition and then put it all back together into a mutated but totally real new form. The structure, as it is, is down to Blier's skill at thinking outside the box. Blier says he wrote the script from the middle onwards, beginning with a fantasising scenario on Mozart, and even

46

contemplating the idea of having an actor portray Mozart during the scenes where Raoul and Stephane muse and dream of the great composer. Though this was abandoned, Mozart's music was to become an essential part of the film, blending seamlessly with Georges Delerue's Cesar Award winning score.

"The idea came to me to make a film about two imbeciles who speak about Mozart as they would about soccer," Blier recalled. "I wrote the scene very quickly, and it appears just as I wrote it then in the film."

Blier had Depardieu and Dewaere in mind for these two afore mentioned imbeciles from the start, having already won great acclaim with them as the two leads in 1974's Going Places. Again, the pair work wonderfully together, at first having conflicts but by the midway point becoming close, if not like brothers, and as in Going Places when it gets going, even dressing in matching clothes. Dewaere embodies the nervy and obsessive intellectual with ease, a mile away from the nasty brute he portrayed in Going Places. It's one of the finest performances from his all too brief film career (he committed suicide in 1982 at the age of 35). Depardieu, again, is marvellous here, playing a curious blend of cuckold and chauvinist, a man who will do anything to "please" his wife but also insist that he knows best when it comes to her happiness. Essentially loaning her to another man, he is a misogynist through and through, another rough and ready male who, though becoming more sophisticated as he begins to appreciate Mozart, seems to degenerate into an even more primitive being as he sees his wife fall for the purer boy he is bitterly jealous of. In a very difficult role, Carole Laure excels, perfecting the bored female put-upon by two old fashioned men, craving a man (in this case, boy) who will let her be who she is. The film may have been accused of being sexist (in the US the Village Voice called it "extraordinarily misogynous by any standards"), but it is more a study of sexism, with Laure's character ultimately getting one up on both Raoul and Stephane in the end.

Rather unexpectedly, it was a smash in America, no doubt because of its Oscar win. When it screened at the New York Film Festival, it was both booed and applauded. Critics either loved it or seemed to find it too bizarre and curious. Pauline Kael, the high priestess of American film criticism, said it made her "unreasonably happy", while Time Out claimed it to be "erratic and often hilarious. Somewhere in all this chaos, the movie firmly puts the boot into mainstream French comedy, substituting absurd and amiable bad taste for the intellectual rigor mortis of which Parisians are so proud." Though they had a point, and indeed Blier's film is a savage beating of the clichéd French comedy, it also exists on its own merit as an engaging, anarchic story which does away with all conventions and creates a sub genre of its own. As good as Depardieu and the others in the cast are, one can't help but feel it is Blier's show entirely.

In an interview with the Washington Post in 1979, Blier said "in France people don't laugh very much at it. For example, when a 13-year-old child gets a 25-year-old woman pregnant, for me that's funny. But in France, they say, 'No, that's impossible. Invariably, you shock some people and stimulate others. When everyone agrees, that's a very bad sign. As a filmmaker, it's best to stretch yourself to your limits. Handkerchiefs' is my favourite of my films so far, and in appearance, yes, it is more whimsical and less abrasive, less political than Going Places. Yet, really I think Handkerchiefs is the more subversive film. In Going Places, where the two men steal cars and hold up picnickers and force women to submit to them, the provocation is visible. Handkerchiefs, on the other hand, is a very soft, very seductive film. But, if you look carefully, all the traditional values are upset here: the couples, the family, maternity."

Though eager to follow his inspiration and go against clichés, he also noted that the film had no message. "I detest messages, false messages perhaps; I like to play with false messages." He did however feel that he was a man qualified to explore women's problems, given he was never a macho singleton and when making the film was married with a child. He did however add that a man should never deny his masculinity. The key to Blier's views on men and women is balance; he clearly thought the exaggerated and hysterical aspects of feminism were absurd, and that extreme machismo was totally out of order. "The men in Handkerchiefs aren't exactly idiots," Blier commented, "but they come pretty close to that. They're very intelligent in their hearts, but more fragile than the woman in their heads. In their own petty way, these two men try to revolutionize things, and the result is catastrophic."

In redefining the French farce, Blier highlights the shortcoming of both sexes, but punctuates his musings with pure surrealism, the idea that everything which happens, no matter how seemingly out of the ordinary, should be accepted as mundane. Fans of Depardieu will be delighted, as it is certainly one of the strongest efforts from his whole varied and rich filmography, as well as one of the finest films he has ever been a part of.

A 2019 retrospective review in the LA Times summed it up thus: "And yet the movie's style is pure deadpan — bored, even, at times, which in a way creates its own blackly humorous fizz regarding our taste for exhaustive sexual escapades, endless psychologizing and the timeless (tired?) allure of the unfathomable object of desire. (Were the signposts of the French New Wave Blier's eye-poking target?) Get Out Your Handkerchiefs may not shock the way it once did, but it remains the purest expression of Blier's comic métier, treating naughty ideas with the straightest of faces."

Buffet Froid (1979)

BUFFET FROID (1979)

The teaming of Bertrand Blier and Gerard Depardieu, in its many varied forms, has always produced films of an extraordinary and unique quality. They first worked together on 1974's Going Places, before earning more world wide notice for Get Your Handkerchiefs Out in 1977. Buffet Froid, released in 1979, is often seen as their finest collaboration and is sometimes ranked as one of the greatest French films of all time (Time Out for instance, placed it in their top 50). A jagged, unpredictable and fearlessly surrealistic experience, Buffet Froid is a film like no other and one can honestly say that there is nothing to which you can compare it, not even other Blier works. Considering the success he had enjoyed before its release, makes it something of a surprise that Blier's Buffet Froid was so misunderstood upon release and enjoyed only a modest amount of success. What is not surprising however, is how it's built up such a healthy cult following in the past couple of decades.

Depardieu is at his most paradoxically appealing and anonymous as Tram, an unemployed no-hoper whose life begins to change beyond all recognition one night when he chances upon a man in the subway. Sitting beside him, with no one else around, he presents the man the knife he conceals on his person and asks him to take it, before he does something silly with it. Irritated, the man reluctantly takes the blade and places it on a seat beside him. When the two men look round however, the knife has vanished into thin air. After the stranger leaves on a train arriving at that pivotal moment, Depardieu's hopeless Tram walks off aimlessly. Later in the night he passes the man in a tunnel, and sticking bloodily out of his belly as he lays against the wall is Tram's own blade. Confused, Tram heads home to the apartment block where only he and his wife live, and upon his return tries to tell her about the murder in the subway while eating his late night dinner. Informed by his wife that a man has moved into the flat above them, Tram pays him a late night visit. Learning he is a chief inspector, Tram becomes animated and tells Insp. Morvandiau (played by Bernard Blier) of the murder, but the cop wants nothing to do with it, telling him to go home and that he is spoiling his relaxing evening. From here on, the film goes from one irrational twist to another, with all logic and reason non existent as Tram's odyssey becomes wilder and wilder. The other characters include a creepy lady-killer (played by Jean Carmet) who adds Tram's wife to his list of murders, and then, along with the cop and a widow of a man Tram himself ends up slaying (named Genevieve, played by Genevieve Page), becomes an active member of this unlikely gang who find themselves stumbling through an increasingly bizarre chain of events.

Blier's film is an undeniable out and out comedy. Though occasionally shocking, he resists explicit imagery or language this time, avoiding the confrontational outrage of Going Places and instead succeeding in bringing a Surrealist masterpiece painting to life before our eyes. As with Blier's best work, a point is being made beneath the stylised surface; the city is an animal, an unforgiving beast which conjures nightmares and turns all humans into amoral, soulless beings, confused by their lives and unable to make sense of those they come into contact with. The buildings are ugly, angular, threatening, and the neighbourhoods are bleak, unfriendly, the kind of places you would avoid if you had any sense. Indeed, Blier's city is a relentless, unforgiving place, a scrap yard of urban decay and human bewilderment.

Blier blends styles and themes to create a masterwork of his own, no doubt influenced by the great Luis Bunuel (especially in the matter-of-fact presentation of the Surrealism, all played out with straight faces and without cartoonish exaggerations), but also conjuring up a paranoiac mood that could easily and fairly be described as Kafka-

52

esque. Though there is no trial, one thinks of Kafka's masterpiece due to the relentlessness and cold distance between the characters and their harsh environments. As with true Surrealism, as its creator and "pope" Andre Breton insisted upon, the characters do not react to the absurdities of their situation, but treat them as ordinary and expected.

Despite the film's detours into the truly bizarre and quite often the macabre, Buffet Froid remains uproariously good fun. This is thanks not only to Blier's script, but also the wonderful performances. Bernard Blier is unsettlingly good as the Inspector, a man who represents the law but bends it to his liking and reacts in the opposite manner to what one might expect when he chances upon, or is presented with a crime. Carmet is very convincing as the sneaky killer, a man who cannot resist killing if he happens to be alone with a woman. Though clearly demented, he seems to be the only one who knows just how alienating and dangerous a place the city is, and is also the only man who knows how to express his disenchantment with the urban experience.

Depardieu is our eyes and ears through this increasingly contorted but strangely more and more acceptable trip into the unknown. This is another one of his lay about lost souls, in the same line as the small time thug of Loulou, the curious motorcyclist of Maitresse and the fiendish crook of Going Places. He perfectly nails the mood, a man at first puzzled by the turn of events but increasingly accepting of it, expectant even by each new revelation waiting around the corner. It's worth noting of course that the one event which kick starts this descent into non-logic is not even recalled by the perpetrator, namely the murder of the stranger in the subway by the blade of Tram. Only at the end, when he is forced to face up to what he has done, does he acknowledge the event as his own doing. The performance is a tour de force because Depardieu makes it all look so natural, never reacting to the scenarios he is faced with. A lesser actor could not have pulled it off with such style.

Critics at the time, especially in America, were lost in the madness. The New York Times, clearly puzzled, wrote "Buffet Froid is well titled. It's a meal composed entirely of side-dishes. There's no main course, and when the meal is over, you're still waiting for something serious to eat. The movie is a collection of random sketches in the service of no dominant idea."

Despite such write-ups, Blier's film is now a classic. Time Out, writing of the film in 2012, declared it a "rigorously absurd contemporary film noir," adding that though it introduced every trademark of the genre, it resisted providing the explanations or motivations of them.

Buffet Froid is one of the true highlights of Depardieu's huge filmography, a film which should forever remain readily available for any film buff who may be lucky enough to stumble upon it on their journey through French cinema.

THE LAST METRO (1980)

Though people popularly believe that Francois Truffaut's artistic peak was during the French New Wave boom of the late fifties and early sixties, with classic films like The 400 Blows and Jules and Jim, I argue that some of his best work was made during the wave's resurgence in the early 80s. Shortly before his untimely death in 1983, Truffait made three extraordinary films, the first of these being 1980s The Last Metro, the second part in his proposed trilogy on the performing arts.

The film concerns a Parisian theatre still operating during German's occupation of France. The Montmatre was formally run by Lucas Stciner, a Jewish theatre director, who is now hiding underground in the basement as his wife, Marion Stciner (played by Catherine Deneuve), runs the establishment and stars as leading lady in their new production. Bernard Grainger (Gerard Depardieu), a womanising young actor, is cast as the lead, and Marion unexpectedly begins to develop feelings for him. As Lucas listens through the vents and writes down directorial ideas for later inspection, the anti-Semite theatre critic Daxiat begins to sniff around, and on top of organising the running of the troupe, Marion has to deal with unannounced visits from the Nazis who wish to examine the premises, including the basement, where her husband, who she is clearly falling out of love with, is kept secret. After Grainger beats up Daxiat in the street when he gives them a bad review (disgustingly highlighting inherent "Jewishness" in the play), it becomes clear he is part of the French Resistance. Will Bernard's fiery personality rouse suspicion and attract the attention of the Nazis, thus blowing Lucas Steiner's cover? As the plot thickens, and friction escalates between the characters, the film becomes more tense, often frustratingly so, as it reaches its climax.

Though Jules and Jim is often picked out as Truffaut's long lasting masterpiece, his seminal offering to the world, I personally believe The

Last Metro deserves more credit. He had wanted to make a film on the French occupation for some time, having been inspired by both the memoirs of actor Jean Marais, and his own uncle and grandfather, who were both caught during the actual era when they were smuggling messages across borders. Truffaut went looking for actors in September of 1979, immediately thinking of Catherine Deneuve as Marion, for whom he wrote the part. When Deneueve agreed to play the role, Truffaut knew he had to cast a formidable actor opposite her, someone who could create believable tension and embody the more Jack the Lad traits of Bernard. He knew Depardieu was the man for the job, but it took some time to convince Gerard to sign up, for he was initially unconvinced that he would enjoy working with Francois, as he admitted he did not like his style. Eventually however, and thankfully, Depardieu was won over.

The fact Depardieu came on board was vital to the success of the film, for it is hard to imagine the film working, or the tension between Bernard and Marion being so convincing, without Gerard's rustic edginess. Deneuve, as appealing as ever, is both radiant and beautiful as Marion, a wonderful characterisation of a powerful, steadfast woman who is also a star of the stage and screen. Playing an actress from another era must be a challenge, but Deneuve pulls it off, playing a woman who is already a myth of the silver screen and pulls in the punters. Her sexiness, as Lucas becomes a strange hermetic father-like figure in her life, is matched by Gerard's slight air of unpredictability and danger. Here is an actor of inspired spontaneity and magic at his early best.

Truffaut establishes true suspense, but resists Hitchcockian techniques and manipulated tension, denying the fall back on dramatic music, conventional scenes of snooping Nazis only just missing sight of their Jewish man-on-the-run. The Last Metro is remarkable because it is gripping and full of tension, but it never resorts to clichés and familiarities. It's simply a good story, establishing believable and likeable (in some cases, detestable) characters who you care about in the trust sense. This is where the film becomes compulsively watchable, having you on the end of your seat, not due to the application of well practised film techniques, but straight forward story telling.

The Last Metro is a truly immaculate film, as close to perfect as you could get. It's a rich and rewarding experience which boasts wonderful, grounded performances, stunning sets and beautiful costumes. It is a masterwork in the truest sense, thanks to the wonderful cast, but most of all for Truffaut's assured control of the whole piece.

It was a big hit in Truffaut's native France as well as over the world, particularly in America, where it made three million dollars in profit. It won ten awards at the Cesars, including Best Picture, while Truffaut won Best Director and Deneuve and Depardieu were rewarded for their fine acting. It also garnered nominations for Best Foreign Language Film at the Oscars and the Golden Globes.

Reviews were almost universally glowing. Though Roger Ebert found it overly involved with the goings on of the theatrical sorts and neglectful of the war outside and the presence of the Nazis, he was perhaps missing the point. Truffaut's film is a microcosm of the period, following a group of people ensuring the show goes on despite the world being in turmoil. That is, of course, the point, with the Nazis secondary to the predicaments which the actors - and the director downstairs of course - find themselves facing.

Other critics loved it, with Vincent Canby declaring it at the time as "a dazzlingly subversive work". These days however, few see it as one of Truffaut's strongest works, though I personally feel it to be among his most involving and assured films, if not his finest work. Many modern reviewers see it as largely hollow, a pretty film with very little to say, concerned with minor instances in a world full of action away from the theatre boards. Notcoming.com wrote, "True, the skilled and subtle performances of Deneuve, Depardieu and Heinz Bennent keep the film from becoming too overwrought, but its problem is really that it never becomes enough of anything: the wandering from genre to genre ultimately becomes tiresome, and undermines the very precise period feel that Truffaut captures."

It seems odd to think that a film which swept the Cesars forty years ago is now largely sidelined, but sadly that is the case with The Last Metro. It is indeed a shame, and one hopes its reputation makes a turnaround in the years to come.

LOULOU (1980)

Gerard Depardieu continued to inspire directors as the new decade came in, and in 1980 he took the lead role in a film directed and co-written by Maurice Pialat, one of the greatest and most important filmmakers in the history of French cinema. Again, Depardieu was to give a primal, almost animal-like performance as a primitive male often on the wrong side of the law, but this time he was matched by a formidable woman (as in Maitresse from 1976), not a mere object for his taking, but a vital person in her own right. The woman in question, of course, was Isabelle Huppert; the film, the brilliant Loulou.

The film begins with Nelly (Huppert) meeting and dancing with Loulou (Depardieu) in a club, a flirtatious interaction which is interrupted by her husband, Andre (played by Guy Marchand), who owns an advertising firm for which Nelly works. Clearly put out by her lust for the dangerous looking stranger, and indeed troubled by Nelly's apparent fondness for this prime alpha male, Andre argues with her in the club about her flirtations. It is clear the pair's relationship has been struggling for some time, and that a split, or indeed an infidelity of a more spontaneous kind, was unavoidable. Nelly spends the night with Loulou, who we learn is an aimless petty crook who squats in dingy lodgings with two friends and makes a living from small time crime. The two become closer and Nelly leaves Andre for him, though Andre continues to keep her in employment, somewhat encouraging his own masochistic qualities, torturing himself by hearing of her lurid activities with the layabout Loulou. As the new relationship deepens, they move in together, her paying his way (he is, of course, broke and unemployed) firstly in a hotel, then a basic flat that fits their needs. She then falls pregnant and begins to be introduced to the people in Loulou's life, his mother and more turbulent friends and in laws. Considering her future with this man lacking in any aspiration, and also still attached to her former employer and lover, Nelly faces a predicament, and it is up to her (and only her) to make sense of the complex emotions of her new life. Is it viable to have a baby with this man in such an unfriendly atmosphere? When she finds herself in the middle of a dramatic family incident involving a loaded shotgun, she has her question answered for her.

Loulou may be forty years old, but a modern day viewing of it proves the film has not aged a day. It is staggeringly raw, raggedly filmed so that it feels like we are there amongst the characters, facing the choices Nelly has to make alongside her. When proceedings turn dangerous, we feel at risk ourselves. Much of this is down to Pialat's filming choices, keeping scenes in long, simple takes and following characters through rooms, corridors and down streets, tracking them as they quarrel, drink in the bar they so often end up in (after all, one person notes, there is nothing else to do), get into scrapes, partake in sleazy or occasionally affectionate sex, act out burglaries, or confront one another unflinchingly. The script, by Pialat and Ariette Langmann, is straight forward and engaging, keeping you concerned, troubled even, with lives that you might otherwise have no interest in.

A large part of the movie's success and appeal is of course down to the performances. Huppert is wonderful as Nelly, a young woman facing a paradox and having to choose between two males; one an always available man who will make love to her, spend time with her, but offer no conversation of depth or meaning and prove to have no desire to work or do anything worthwhile; the other a man who owns a successful business, can keep her employed, and with whom she shares interests in literature and art. Yet Andre bores her, and she does not mind telling him. He may have goals and aspirations, but he is never there physically or emotionally; and when he is, by his own admission, he is too tired to have sex or do much at all. Loulou, though a directionless wastrel, prone to drinking with buddies, having casual flings with women on the side and choosing a life of petty crime over hard and honest work, is there in truest sense, his animal magnetism understandably appealing to a woman who craves physical satisfaction and wishes to feel needed, loved and desired all at the same time. Huppert embodies this struggle perfectly, making her characterisation seem totally natural and effortless.

Depardieu is staggeringly good, a primitive male always on the look out for flirtation, sexual gratification, a quick steal, an opportunity for fun or an excuse to fight. He is constantly shifty, the work shy chancer through and through; raw, rough around the edges and a live wire, very much in love with his sordid life though unwilling to do much more than steal, fuck and drink his nights away. Depardieu is wonderful here, a gift to any director and clearly a total natural. A man who began his own life in less than savoury and conventional ways, Depardieu is able to get beneath the skin of this urban survivor, the street wise hustler more than at home on the seedy sidewalks and in the dodgy bars.

Loulou works on two levels, as any serious art film should; on the surface is a compelling and often exciting tale of two people in love, with a third off to one side, left abandoned but perversely drawn into the details of his former lover's new life. Beneath this of course is a study of class differences in the urban environment. Huppert, as one learns from her suited, snobbish brother (who comes to hassle Depardieu into getting a decent job and even offers to start up a cafe for him so that he will give his sister a good life) comes from a more well to do middle class family. She makes her views of Depardieu's more rough and ready status clear indeed; when they are two lovers living on the edge, she adores their vital life together, overlooking his shortcoming and seeing them as rugged charms and he as a hungry male; when, however, she sees the truth of his daily life and their inevitable destiny together (not to mention when she is sat silent and uncomfortable at Loulou's loud family gathering), she could not feel more aware of the vast differences between them. Loulou works as a slice of life drama, a glimpse into early 80s feminism, the class divide and the urban struggle; but for the most part it succeeds as a very enjoyable story, one acted superbly by two French icons at their youthful best.

Loulou has become a cult classic down the years and is now considered a seminal European film of the time and one of Pialat's finest works. When it was placed at number 67 in Time Out's Top 100 French Films of All Time, they called it "a challenging, absorbing example of the awkward beauty of Pialat." concluding that it has a habit of "haunting you long after it has ended." Pialat earned a Best Director at Cannes that year, but the film was shunned at various award ceremonies where it should have received more attention.

CHOICE OF ARMS (1981)

Gerard Depardieu found himself alongside Catherine Deneuve once again in Alain Corneau's gripping Choice of Arms, which also starred his future Jean de Florette co-star Yves Montand. With a sharp script from Alain and co-writer Michel Grisolia, it concerns Noel (Montand), a retired gangster who now cares for horses on his country estate, living an idyllic life with Nicole (Deneuve), his beautiful wife. Meanwhile, three crooks appear to be in a spot of trouble, and after attracting the attention of the police, the wildest of the three, Mickey (Depardieu) shoots a cop dead. Going into an abandoned wasteland, their car is besieged by bullets from a rival criminal. The third crook flees, leaving only Mickey and the older Serge. After injuring Serge, the gun man gets away, and Mickey and Serge end up at Noel's home, Serge recuperating in one of the spare beds. But through no fault of his own, Noel becomes entangled in a murky plot, the kind of which he thought he had left behind him in his long gone crime days. The police turn up at Noel's house, so Mickey hides out in Paris with a friend, but he accuses Noel of informing on him. It is here where things turn particularly nasty.

Choice of Arms is a compelling crime thriller, with a healthy pace, suspense and plenty of tension, but in true European fashion it is not exploitative, violent for the sake of it or cliché ridden. It is, in fact, an in-depth character study of what people will reduce themselves to, an exploration of humanity in the truest sense. It is, therefore, a film to enjoy for the performances, even if the plot itself is engaging.

Montand, a true icon of French cinema, is solid as Noel, a self assured man seeing his paradise slipping away with the arrival of these two unwanted, shady characters, while the gorgeous Deneuve is as effective as ever, perfect as a calm wife who personifies, with her smooth exterior and gentle way, the fact that Noel's life had certainly improved since giving up the gangster life.

Depardieu, however, still in his transitional phase when he moved from playing streetwise hoods to more varied characters, gives the finest effort, a real loose cannon portrayed with high voltage unpredictability. He is at his most exciting and vital, a remarkable screen presence whenever he appears. He is in fact the first person to appear in the film, wearing his blue coat, shiftily fleeing trouble and climbing over a wall, trouble from the very start. As in many of his pictures from this period, Gerard has some remarkable scenes, such as when he kills the police man and instantly realises what he has done, and the wonderful sequence where he runs freely, almost child-like, with Noel's horses. He is, though it's become a cliché in itself, a force of nature. This lonely drifter, not unlike his Buffet Froid character, is frightened boy as much as dangerous criminal. But he is a psycho, one of Depardieu's most deadly in his gallery of faces. Again, it's the combination of coarseness and vulnerability, the harsh physicality combined with emotional fragility.

Choice of Arms is a great film, a standout of 80s French cinema and, like Police (1985) and other crime films to come out of Europe in that decade, avoids giving us pointless, flashy thrills with an emphasis on characters and nuance. It's essential for fans of all three lead actors.

THE WOMAN NEXT DOOR (1981)

Depardieu was back under the direction of Francois Truffait once again with 1981's The Woman Next Door, now considered one of the most important French films of the decade. Though Francois would make one more picture before his death, namely Vivement dimanche, in many ways The Woman Next Door is his true swan song, his final bow. And what a final bow it is, a compelling, masterful, beautifully acted tale of love and infatuation.

When the film begins, we are introduced to the seemingly content world of Bernard (Depardieu), who lives with his wife and child in a beautiful house in a rural village near Grenoble. When a new couple move into the house next door, Bernard is shocked to learn that the woman is Mathilde (Fanny Ardant), an old flame with whom he enjoyed a turbulent affair years earlier. It having been a rough break up, there looms a strange tension between the pair. At first, Bernard commits to ignoring Mathilde, putting her out of his mind and treating her with quiet disdain. After a while though, he relents and they begin to be friendly again, unavoidably leading to a passionate affair. They regularly meet up in a hotel to make love, and as the affection deepens, it is clear that both Bernard and Mathilde are meant to be together, even if their union is ultimately doomed. They attempt to stick with their complacent but ultimately unrewarding home lives, but the pull between them is too strong. Following a series of events which mount upheaval in their social circle, the emotion becomes unbearable for the two adulterers, and the film ends with a powerful and tragic climax which is purely devastating and, I have to say, totally unexpected on first viewing.

The Woman Next Door is a film which masterfully builds frustration and tension, both lead characters experiencing a shake-up they would not have foreseen only a matter of weeks before the film begins, but one they sadly could not have avoided. The sheer chance of her moving in next door, rocking his world and highlighting his quiet discontentment, was of course slim, but the pair were destined to be drawn together once more. We learn their split was ugly, and that Mathilde thought him a terrifying and jealous man. But Bernard is clearly infatuated with her (he always was), obsessed even, and totally wrapped up in this graceful and beautiful woman. She too is obsessed, and her love for him heightens to a level so that she can barely contain it or hang on to her sanity. This is a tale of love as madness, madness as love, and how the two often go hand in hand. This irrational desire takes over everything and leads the two people, whose lives looked so simple before the affair, into a heartbreaking but hauntingly beautiful destiny.

Depardieu was highly acclaimed for the performance and today people see his work with Truffaut as some of his finest. So natural as the everyday father, he heads to work in the morning (a curious job, instructing people on small replicas of tankers in the local pond) in suit and tie, dashing to the car after kissing his wife and son goodbye. Holding it all together, he begins to unravel, showing that wild side Mathilde has spoken of to her husband (played with restraint by Henri Garcen). While the love he enjoys with his wife is enviable and pure, the one he endures or indeed suffers with Mathilde is bad, needy, unhealthy; hungry if not starving, and weirdly parasitic. They yearn but are not content with enjoying their time together, for they simply have to devour and consume one another. It is love as destroyer, a love to be feared. Ardant is simply wonderful as Mathilde, harbouring all her complexities in her dark and mysterious eyes, ready to crack at any minute. This cosy middle class world is coming apart at the seams, and Depardieu and Ardant convey this wonderfully.

Speaking to the Guardian recently, Ardant mentioned first reading the script for the film and being stunned. It has also seems to have had a lasting effect on her. "When I read the synopsis of The Woman Next Door I was completely stunned by the idea that you could die of love. The only thing I've ever believed in, at the risk of seeming sentimental, is love. If I'm at a boring dinner I always ask the man next to me, whether he's an ambassador or the president of the Republic: Do you love your wife? It's the only interesting subject."

Shot with expertise by William Lubtchansky, it is perverse that this dark story of obsession looks so beautiful, so picturesque. Even as the obsession becomes sickening for them, we are in awe of the cinematography, the graceful direction and the seamless editing.

The Woman Next Door did well in France and also garnered some acclaim, though it did not sweep the Cesars like The Last Metro, Truffaut's previous film. Reviews overseas were mixed, and not everyone understood what Truffaut was going for. Roger Ebert wrote that "Truffaut is on record as one of the greatest admirers of Hitchcock, and The Woman Next Door is a profoundly Hitchcockian film in that its real subjects are guilt, passion and terrible consequences of a sin that starts out small. The two lovers are criminals in the moralistic sense, of course, adulterers, cheaters, liars, as practised at concealing their emotions as a veteran con man. Truffaut does a brilliant job of giving us surface images that are almost starkly simple, while beneath the surface there's a labyrinthine tangle of passions."

The New York Times wrote of the two stars, "Mr. Depardieu is not only the busiest French film actor alive at the moment, he also must be the most resourceful and compelling. His Bernard is charming and loving on the surface and an emotional bandit beneath. Fanny Ardant, a stage actress new to films, is perfectly cast as Mathilde. She brings to the role no psychological baggage from other appearances, so that she really is as mysterious to us as she is to Bernard."

The Woman Next Door is certainly one of Truffaut's finest films, and features two mesmerising displays of acting from Depardieu and

Ardant. An uncomfortable though still rewarding picture, it shows, though in an exaggerated fashion, what many people are hiding beneath their seemingly perfect, ideal lives.

THE RETURN OF MARTIN GUERRE (1982)

Among the most engaging and lasting films Depardieu made in the 1980s at the height of his fame was The Return of Martin Guerre, a graceful minor masterpiece from director Daniel Vigne, a parable on identity which boasts fine performances and a gripping and quite often very surprising script.

Based on true events, or at least inspired by them, it is set in a 16th century French village. The tale begins with the marriage of Martin Guerre and Bertrande de Rois, a young couple in their late teens. When Martin proves unable to impregnate his wife, he brings shame on her before the whole village. One day he leaves, and as time goes on it appears he will not return. Much occurs in his absence; for one, Martin's parents pass away, and his wife's mother marries his uncle Pierre. Nine years later, with his infant son grown up, Martin returns in the form of Gerard Depardieu, broader, bulkier and more grown up than the Martin Guerre they once knew. At first the village accepts him with open arms, and if anything young Bertrande prefers this new man to the other. When some vagabonds arrive in town to sleep in a barn, Martin brings them food. It is then the tramps inform Martin's cousin that the man claiming to be Martin Guerre is actually a man called Arnaud. Martin, they say, was at war with them and Arnaud, and lost his leg in battle. Eventually things begin to change in the town and the people soon doubt the true identity of Depardieu. He is put on trial, one which seems to be going the right way for Guerre and his contented wife, but shifts in the opposite direction when a most unexpected visitor arrives in the court room.

Director Daniel Vigne directed and produced the film, and also worked on the screenplay with historian Natalie Zemon Davis, who being an expert on early French history, worked as a consultant on set and later released a book about the case. Her knowledge of the period no doubt enriched the film and enhanced its authenticity (indeed, one can almost smell the manure and mud), but the key to the success of this film is the screenplay and its clever construction. It begins with authorities questioning the grown up Bertrande, played by the great Nathalie Baye, all about the disappearance and subsequent arrival of the new Martin Guerre. As the plot catches up with events, half way through the film, it is revealed that those interrogating her are involved in the case against this so-called imposter, and from there afterwards the film is set amidst the gripping trial. The dialogue is excellent and the direction is both assured and straight forward. The performances however are something else entirely. The whole cast dazzle and fit into their roles as if they were really born in that long ago era. Baye is quietly brilliant, a totally convincing wife of the era, and one who being abandoned by one husband then gets a second chance with a better man, one keen on providing for and satisfying her, and happily going along with the charade.

Depardieu had been good before this, but there seems to be an extra dimension to this performance which heightens it above even the finest work he had done up to the early 80s. If one looks back at the hoodlums and thugs of Loulou, Going Places and Maitresse, the straight forward working man of 1900, the resistance fighting actor of The Last Metro and the obsessed adulterer of The Woman Next Door, what he does here is slightly different. There is a special kind of charisma on display, a working man through and through, but also a magnet to the people around him, the very definition of a "decent" man. The contradiction of course is in the fact he is a faker, a charlatan, living the life of another man with whom he fought the war, a man who lost a leg for his country. In his defence, he makes a better life for Bertrande than the real Guerre - a more defensive and insecure man - ever could. He even asks the court if it's such a bad thing for a man to make an abandoned woman happy once again, but he gets little support in his case.

Though the whole cast are authentic, Depardieu looks as if he has come out of an old painting, a completely believable peasant of the Francis I era. In his book Innocent, Depardieu says he studied the paintings of Hieronymus Bosch and observed the hunched stances of the people in them, their contorted faces and disjointed manners, never upright. The studious detail is evident in this most persuasive characterisation. Not only does he convince us he is the real Martin Guerre, he tricks us into thinking he's come straight from the 16th century. One must add that it never feels like Depardieu is acting, neither as Martin or Arnauld, but getting under the skin of his latest character. The word natural doesn't begin to do this work justice.

Though The Return of Martin Guerre works in its own right as a convincing and compelling story, there are certain points raised here about a society which, though hundreds of years in the past, still holds resonance to modern viewers. The idea of identity itself, what it is to be one person and one person only, to attempt to convince others, makes us question the individual within society. There are also points about the church, so venomous against a man who dares to dishonour a marriage, as well as the concept of family. After all, it is his family who happily mocked the real Guerre until he left, and then chastised the fake one who came in his place. Yes this is set in 1500s France, but some of the themes seem weirdly relevant.

The Return of Martin Guerre was highly acclaimed at the time and attracted various award nominations, though it won next to none. It was only a minor success in Depardieu's native France but was a sizeable hit across the globe.

The New York Times gave it a rave review, it being a hit in America, and praised Depardieu's work: "Gerard Depardieu, who has recently been in danger of becoming a parody of his own striking screen personality, is superb as the returned veteran. The hulking Depardieu looks the way a 16th-century peasant should look or, as Mr. Vigne has said in an interview, he's one of the few contemporary actors who wouldn't be a sight gag in the period costumes. His is a beautifully executed performance, its power always controlled and not, as sometimes happens with Mr. Depardieu, exercised for its own flamboyant sake."

If one were to pick ten films of Depardieu's to remember him by, then surely, The Return of Martin Guerre should be there. Anyone unconvinced of the man's true power, perhaps confused by such a reputation when only aware of, say, The Man in the Iron Mask or the Asterix and Obelix films (though I'm a fan, while others aren't), should witness the natural and controlled charm he exudes here. A truly wonderful film.

MOON IN THE GUTTER (1983)

There are a lot of curious and even bizarre films in the vault of 1980s cinema, but Moon in the Gutter is certainly one of the strangest. It isn't because particularly weird things happen in a contrived or forced manner to make the film wacky for the sake of it, but because it has a mood quite unlike anything else, and a certain satisfaction in wallowing in its own surrealistic oddness.

Moon in the Gutter stars Gerard Depardieu as Gerard, a young man who works on the docks and is haunted by the rape and subsequent suicide of his sister. Tormented, he repeatedly returns to the alley where it happened, seeing a puddle of her blood, luminous and otherworldly, as a reminder of the hellish incident. Unable to find the perpetrator, Gerard drinks his days away with the losers who frequent the local bar, and lives with a woman who may or may not be a lady of the night. He is trapped, but some salvation comes with the arrival of the beautiful Loretta (Nastassja Kinski), a rich girl who arrives in a vintage Ferrari to photograph the workers of the docks and the lowlifes Gerard surrounds himself with. The girl clearly reminds him of his dead sister, but can she pull him away from the dead end alley he exists in?

Moon in the Gutter is compulsively watchable, even though it would more than likely puzzle most casual viewers. Based on David Goods' novel, it was directed by Jean-Jacques Beineix, who though suffering poor reviews and bad box office with Moon in the Gutter would go on to score a cult hit with his next film, Betty Blue. This film though, as forgotten as it is, should not be overlooked. It is far from perfect, and often feels like a mish mash of genres (erotica, thriller, fantasy, drama, weird sci-fi, dark comedy, even action at one point), but has a moody, creepy atmosphere which pulls you in. Even when it is clear not very much is going to happen and that the narrative is non existent, Moon in the Gutter keeps you hooked... or it did me at least. There is a blend of reality and dream throughout, and the viewer becomes unable to separate what is actually occurring in the so called real world and in Gerard's troubled mind. Bordering on nightmarish at times, it's a grim experience but one which remains strangely satisfying. In a weird way, even when it's over, you almost fee like putting it on again, if not to merely make sense of it, but to wallow once again in its grottiness.

The direction is wonderful, the vibe noirish, and the performances abstractly strong. Depardieu himself is as solid as ever, in a typical manner swinging from sensitive and tortured one minute, to violent and animalistic the next. Depardieu later said that it was meeting Francois Truffaut that moved him from his bold hooligan roles of the seventies and into a decade of variety, but in many ways Moon in the Gutter feels like one of his seventies films, much edgier than the more mainstream fare he was a part of in the 1980s. It is a very strong performance and he holds the film together as best he can. Kinski, striking as ever, is wonderfully glamorous, and one has to mention the ever excellent Dominique Pinon as Frank, Gerard's drunken loser friend.

Moon in the Gutter was speedily buried in time, misunderstood by its critics upon release and relegated to the obscurity vault. It is out there on VHS and foreign DVD, and anyone into off beat films of the 80s, and Depardieu himself of course, should definitely seek this curiosity out.

DANTON (1983)

In 1983 Gerard Depardieu gave another highly acclaimed performance in Danton, winning the National Society of Critics and Montreal World Film Festival awards for Best Actor. In Andrzej Wajda's heavyweight drama, Depardieu portrays French Revolution leader Georges Danton in his final weeks, a devastatingly powerful effort which proved he had even more sides as an actor than even his loyalist supporters might have thought. The previous year he had stunned world audiences as Martin Guerre, but here, portraying a titan of French history, from his struggles to his execution, Gerard proved himself unmatched in world cinema. Perhaps only the great Marcello Mastroianni, still delivering formidable performances in this era, could have come anywhere near him.

It must be stated that, though the picture is about key French history, it is directed by a Polish filmmaker and based on a novel by Stanislawa Przybyszewska, a fellow Pole himself. As a viewer it feels vital, perhaps only personally, that a non-Frenchman should guide such a tale, not suggesting a total distance from the subject but at least one far enough to not feel too connected to the material. This is not a typical Hollywood epic, but a wordier, at times explosively lyrical exploration of a brief period; but it is epic in the truest sense, and wonderfully played out too. Although it sometimes feels like a history lesson and at times might be a challenge or even a slog for less patient viewers, it is a rewarding film. Most of all, it is one to see for the acting, which in all honesty cannot be faulted.

Thanks mostly to the presence of its star, Danton was a commercial hit as well as a critical one. When it saw a US release, to much acclaim, Roger Ebert gave it four out of four, despite its open inaccuracies as far as history was concerned. "Danton is played by Gerard Depardieu," wrote Ebert, "that large, proletarian French actor who is so useful in roles where high-flown emotions need some sort of grounding. He makes his hoarse-voiced, idealistic speeches to the senate sound like a football coach at halftime. This movie may not be an accurate record of the events of 1793 and 1794, and indeed in Paris the critics are up in arms over its inaccuracies. But as a record of the fiery passions and glorious personalities of the revolution, it is absolutely superb."

Even critics who found the film itself hard work could not deny the power of Depardieu's work. Eye For Film wrote, "Depardieu, in the title role, gives a performance, which, if called passionate, would be an understatement. In one impressive courtroom scene, he delivers a lengthy speech in a single uninterrupted take. His rage reaches such a level that he is left for the rest of the film only able to speak in a hoarse whisper. It is an echo that lasts until the final guillotine blade, dripping in blood, falls."

Danton was another opportunity for Depardieu to stretch himself as an actor, to experience another age, another human predicament, a kind of humanity only an actor of his power could even dare to approach.

POLICE (1985)

Gerard Depardieu worked with director Maurice Pialat once again on 1985's Police, five years after their first collaboration together on the rough and raw Loulou. Here, rather than playing a care free small time criminal, he was on the other side of the law, the right side, only his cop is harsh, slightly cynical and not a completely exemplary example to the rest of the force. He plays Mangin, a Marseille based inspector who wants to topple a Tunisian drug ring. He is a tough cop, rough and ready, not afraid of slapping and roughing up the crooks he's arrested, but not above a bit of jaded realism either. However, on this particular case, his stubborn morals are challenged not only by his communications with the criminals themselves, but Noria, played by the beautiful Sophie Marceau, a girlfriend of the head dealer. Slowly, but surely, his fondness for this mysterious woman develops into a strange kind of love, misguided yes, but also unavoidable for Mangin.

As with Loulou, Pialat directs in a fearless style, veering more towards documentary than anything truly cinematic. Indeed, there are no flashy angles, no cleverly worked out shots, but often long tracking ones, the camera following cops and crooks down dull corridors, into offices where typists hammer away at paperwork and the accused are cuffed and taken in and out of rooms. Pialat presents this world, one suspects, as it might have actually been in the mid 1980s. The Marseille police, says one crook, are tougher than the Parisians, and Depardieu and his men prove this time and time again. This is no slick cop thriller, but a gritty, down and dirty portrait of police life and what some officers will do to get results.

Depardieu is toweringly brilliant here, intimidating as can be when at work, slapping criminals, even banging their heads off desks if he wants to, and striking women roughly. Outside the office, when socialising with colleagues, he is good humoured, light, always smiling and popular.

77

But his joviality is superficial and forced. To him, police work is his practise, and he knows all the tricks of the trade. A true professional, he can explode at the arrested at any minute, though one can see the careful theatrics of his performances. His anger works as a way to get answers and confessions. Depardieu embodies this man so well, this professional crime buster, that it's hard to imagine it's the same man who brought to life the thugs of Loulou, The Last Woman and Going Places. He was nominated for a Cesar Award for his work and rightfully won Best Actor at the Venice Film Festival. By the mid 1980s, in giving performances of this quality, Depardieu was the king of French cinema, and was as acclaimed overseas as in his native country. Sophie Marceau, at this stage a rising star, is also brilliant as the oddly appealing Noria.

But this is truly the work of Pialat, who sets the first part of his film up as a frantic exploration of police life, with character faces appearing and disappearing in quick succession, the streets and offices explored in every corner by the camera's probing eye. Only in the second half does it calm down, when Noria and Mangin enter their strange romance. Though Pialat had enjoyed acclaim (and controversy) prior to this, he had not had a major hit yet and Police was his first conscious effort to break out into the mainstream. Whereas other, lesser directors might have relied on cheap action and shoot outs, Pialat focuses on the paperwork, the head aches and confusion of police life, most of it being in the office, not out on the street chasing bad guys down dark alleys. Like Loulou, it unflinchingly goes up close and personal, showing the darkness and light in everyday life. While Loulou focused on a hoodlum and his new girl, Police presents the unpleasant world of the law, and a usually strong willed cop finding himself weakened by a female he cannot resist. His film does not condemn any crook or any cop, and Pialat resists the opportunity to preach or deliver a pretentious message. Instead, he keeps his view out of proceedings and shows us what he sees, and indeed what we would most likely see if a documentary crew, undetected, were showing us the inner workings of the law system.

Pialat naturally encouraged a naturalistic style of acting without posing. He famously hated "American style acting, where every effect is calculated down to the millimetre... the Nicholsons and the Streeps... because it is based entirely on artifice." There is no room for the starry mentality in Police nor any other Pialat film for that matter, and any box office mega star would have been horrified to find himself in a Pialat film devoid of flattering lenses and showy, phony close ups. Police is ragged and raw, a most satisfying experience in a decade which - especially in America - encouraged fakery of the most expensive and dishonest order.

On top of its awards and nominations, Police was a massive commercial success, bringing in nearly two million punters in France alone. It was by far Pialat's biggest hit, and that is perhaps the reason why he hated it so much. This said, it got great reviews upon release. Time Out, recognising its uniqueness, wrote "Pialat is heir to the misanthropic strain in French culture, and dwells at great length on the uncomfortably real. There is no one else who pushes his actors to such uncomfortable extremes. If you want a thriller, then you're in for a rough ride; this is about tension, conflict and hostility, and almost all of it between man and woman."

Police is one of the most important French films of the 1980s, a curio too, because it is a genre piece directed by an auteur, the great Pialat, who raises the cop genre up a level by concerning himself not with the action, the car chases and shoot outs, but with the human beings living their live in this most complex of jungles. An essential stop for an admirer of Depardieu, or anyone curious about exploring what French cinema had to offer in the age of the rise of the blockbuster. If America had Beverly Hills Cop as its typical cop movie, France had Police, and I know which I would choose.

Jean de Florette (1986)

JEAN DE FLORETTE (1986)

Jean de Florette is one of the most celebrated films in the history of European cinema, a most unexpected phenomenon which was not only the most expensive motion picture made in France up that point, but was also the most successful too. Directed by and co scripted by Claude Berri, and based on Marcel Pagnol's novel, Jean de Florette has lost none of its power, charm and devastating impact as the years have gone by.

This wonderful movie is set in a village in Provence, France, in the post war years of the late 1910s. It follows the devious plans of Ugolin (Daniel Auteuil) and his uncle Cesar (Yves Montand), who attempt to buy a piece of property and land from a farmer, knowing that it has its own natural water source and land for Ugolin to begin growing his much desired field of roses, which will bring in large sums of money every year. When the farmer refuses to give up his home, he and Cesar end up in a skirmish, during which the farmer receives a blow to the head and dies. At the funeral, it becomes clear that the land has been inherited by the farmer's sister, who is a former sweetheart of Cesar's. When she too dies, the land goes to her son, Jean Cadoret Gerard Depardieu), a hunchbacked family man who has been working in the big city as a tax collector, but wanting to live a rural life, craving a connection to the natural world, has moved to the sticks. Cesar and his cretinous nephew however are one step ahead of Jean, blocking the water supply to spoil Jean's plans from the outset so he will eventually give up on his dream, sell them the land for cheap and clear off, leaving them with their greedy minded plans to get rich. However, Jean, a kind and warm hearted man with a wife and child, is not going to be giving up easily. He prays for rain during the drought to save his crops, and thinks up all manners of grand schemes to profit off his inherited land. However hard they the scheming uncle and nephew try, they cannot

81

seem to destroy Jean's will power; until of course the tragic and unavoidable occurs.

Much of Jean de Florette is taken up by Jean's relentless efforts to make a good country life for he and his family, and his struggles create an air of desperation, exhaustion even. While the nephew has only half befriended Jean to get inside information, which he then divulges to Cesar, Jean himself sees Ugolian as a decent man. This is more down to Jean's kind heart than anything; for instance, when his daughter comments on Ugolian's ugliness, Jean poetically tells her "sometimes the ugliest exteriors hide the purest souls." Poor Jean though, is unaware of Ugolian's dark greed. Though we are with Jean all the way through his efforts, cheering for him when things go right, depressed when his plans go awry, nothing can compare us for the tragic and utterly heartbreaking finale.

Jean de Florette is the first part in a double bill, followed by Manon de Sources, which was filmed back to back with its predecessor. Budgeted at the equivalent of 17 million dollars, it was a hugely ambitious work and an intimidating undertaking for French cinema, usually accustomed to smaller films from auteurs. It was filmed in Vaucluse, Provence, with houses featuring painted polystyrene fronts to capture the authenticity of the era. They even planted olive trees a full year before filming so they would be growing healthily in time for filming to commence. Shooting for both films took a total of 30 weeks, a staggering amount of time for a French production.

For such varied characters, Berri could not have found a better cast of actors; Montand is utterly bloodless as the arrogant, self centred Cesar, while Auteuil, with prosthetic nose, is utterly vile as the snake like Ugolian, so trustworthy to Jean's face, but a conniving worm of a man as soon as his back is turned. Both are excellent performances, but for me the finest and most revelatory work comes from Depardieu. Up to this point, Gerard had mostly excelled as street wise crooks, harsh small time criminals, chancers and opportunists, though to avoid generalisation he had played a wide variety of outsiders and odd balls. Here though, he is a completely decent man with only naivety to hold him back. While his physical deformity is an immediate distraction (as well as being a talking point for the cruel villagers who do not wish to accept him), we almost instantly forget about it until Jean himself mentions it. A loving father and husband, he has carefully planned out his scheme to live off the soil, breed rabbits and grow his own food, touchingly referring to his guide books every time he has a new genius idea he excitedly wishes to share with the sneaky Ugolian. Depardieu brings out Jean's wide eyed hopefulness, his hopes, his dreams of an idyllic family life in a country cottage. Unfortunately, he is being infiltrated by two vipers, but him being so innocent and pure, trusting of humanity, knows nothing of their sadistic plot to ruin his livelihood. Depardieu is absolutely brilliant throughout, this being perhaps his most likeable character.

On location, crew members recalled that Depardieu kept spirits up by making jokes and playing around, even shouting at aeroplanes flying overhead when they were noisily ruining shots. Despite often not knowing his lines right before action was yelled, he effortlessly became Jean de Florette, the romantic and ultimately tragic hero. Depardieu has often said he does not consider himself an actor and denies even having a method (he lives, he says, and does not act), which makes this transformation - both mental and physical - all the more awe inspiring. Though Gerard himself might roll his eyes at the very idea of it, but his Jean de Florette is a little piece of cinema magic.

Jean de Florette is an unrelenting, often harsh study of human character, a display of greed, selfishness, and how low man will stoop in order to make a little money. If you were to only watch part one, you might think that the message is that bad deeds do not always go noticed or punished. If one views the second chapter, Manon des Sources, one gets the feeling that Berri is delivering a moral of karma, justice and just deserts. Still, the defeat of Cesar and Ugolian in the second film does not lessen the sheer heartache induced by Jean's sad fate.

Jean de Florette was not only a commercial success, it was also praised by critics and award societies. Though only winning one Cesar (Best Actor for Auteuil, much deserved) it was nominated for eight. It won Best Film at the BAFTAS, garnered numerous nominations (Depardieu was acknowledged for Best Supporting Actor there, but unfortunately did not win), and also received top honours from the Moscow Film Festival and US National Board of Review.

Reviews were glowing too, particularly abroad (some French critics thought it mythologized the era), with the film as a whole and the cinematography in particular attracting a considerable amount of acclaim. Many critics noted Depardieu's "dependability" (Roger Ebert), his "hulking screen presence" (Washington Post), while The New York Times said it was "a film like no other you've ever seen." It was an instant classic and remains to this day a masterwork of acting, pacing and direction. In a retrospective piece, Empire Magazine dubbed it, "A simple, elemental tale that makes breaking the heart seem like the easiest and most natural thing a filmmaker can do to his audience. Which, of course, it isn't."

As effective as it is affecting, it is quite simply one of the most involving and emotive films of the 1980s. Yet, as great as it truly is, it's hard to imagine the whole thing without the presence of Depardieu, who elevates proceedings whenever on the screen.

UNDER THE SUN OF SATAN (1987)

Maurice Pialat's Under the Sun of Satan is a very serious, unsettling, unrelenting, intense, but ultimately powerful drama based on the book by Georges Bernanos. This brutal film has no humour or relief whatsoever, but in its combination of controlled direction, stunning photography, meditative pace and assured performances, it's among the most compelling pictures of its era, a moral drama dealing with good and evil, the balance of dark and light powers, and the conflict between God and Satan. Little wonder it won the Palme d'Or at the Cannes Film Festival.

Gerard plays Donissan, a country priest who not only takes his faith seriously (perhaps too seriously for some), but is prone to extreme self punishment. His intense devotion to the church is not only disturbing for the viewer, but also his elder, Menou-Segrais, played with conviction by Pialat himself. Though committed to his religion, Donissan is troubled by the fact that he feels the presence of the devil more than he does God, causing an inner conflict which disturbs those around him, but more so himself. To redeem himself from darkness, he attempts to save a young girl named Mouchette (Sandrine Bonnaire), a troubled soul who uses her flesh to please others but has no self respect. Pregnant to a lover, she shoots him dead with his own shotgun. Though not a suspect in the murder, her self-loathing reaches new heights in the wake of the event. On his way to rescue the girl from her own sins, Donissan has a chilling encounter with a man representing the devil, a haunting figure who convinces Donissan that Satan is in him, in us all in fact. Overcome with dread, Donissan puts his muddled energy into rescuing Mouchette from her sins. But his heavy handed attempts at a redemptive epiphany for the girl are misguided, resulting in a tragedy he could not have foreseen. Racked with guilt, he goes out to see a dying boy and in one of the film's most overpoweringly bold scenes, he lifts

85

the child in the air above his head, only to see him open his eyes and draw breath. He may have saved the child, but at what cost to himself?

People often call this a religious film by a non believer, though in one interview Pialat himself thought it ludicrous to call him an atheist, seeing as it would be paradoxical to feel so strongly about something he supposedly had no belief in. This, then, is not a religious film, but one dealing with faith, the mentality of those with a devotion to the cross, as well as the place of the priest in society (a pillar, one who people choose to believe is a flawless character). Really though, I feel it is about the simple struggle between good and evil, the power of religious belief and the heavy responsibility of being a man of the cloth. The actual power of Depardieu's character is left to ones imagination, whether he really did encounter a devil or just his own personal devil, or really had anything to do with the revival of the child. Either way, Donissan lives through these experiences and we are forced to face them both literally and metaphorically.

One theme, clearly the musing of a non believer, is in the idea that religion does not offer Donissan and his mentor a release from life's agonies, but only deepens their confusion with existence itself. They are not men who have found anything; in fact their faith brings them more questions than answers. While Donissan is in the midst of his struggles with doubt, Menou-Segrais has learned to live with them, aged with some wisdom but no real idea about where he fits into God's plan. Donissan's encounter with the devil, lit in a haunting blue as night nears, seems to be the only moment of truth and understanding, the point where the priest knows that God cannot save him from the devil within himself. Even when reviving the child, he is unsure whether the power within him to perform the act is divine or demonic, a most troubling predicament. Depardieu himself noted in a 2003 interview that the ultimate paradox was the fact that Donissan felt he was an oracle leading sheep, but was in actual fact a lunatic.

Under the Sun of Satan is considered one of Pialat's biggest successes, both artistically as a complete film and in the minds of his public. Though getting the vote for Best Film, it was booed at Cannes. Pialat, undeterred, took to the stage to address his vocal critics, stating, "I won't be untrue to my reputation. I am, above all, happy this evening for all the shouts and whistles you've directed at me; and, if you don't like me, I can tell you that I don't like you either." He held his fist up in determination. Later, asked about his words, he added that he may have been joking, but that didn't mean he liked them either. One can only admire his confidence.

As ever, Pialat directs without fussiness, often following events in long takes, occasionally going in for close ups during moments of importance and capturing the truth of each scene. All this benefits the acting, which is of course tremendous. Pialat was one of Depardieu's mentors, a cantankerous character who, though rubbing many up the wrong way, was always defended by Gerard, who thought Maurice didn't get the attention and acclaim he deserved, while younger, lesser talents were raved about. Depardieu and Pialat worked together a few times, but for me this riveting drama is their finest hour.

Depardieu, in a performance which deserved every possible award going, is a revelation. Gone is the dangerous energy, that charisma and street wise modernity; he is every bit the self flagellating man of God, a troubled soul riddled with doubts and uneasiness. It's a staggering feat of acting, with Depardieu once again displaying his sheer versatility. One New York Times journalist was given a glimpse into the film's editing process. Before a take observed in the editing suite, the writer claimed Depardieu, in full priest gear, had the crew in stitches, mincing and wiggling, playing the clown. As soon as "action" is yelled, writes the reporter, "he is Abbe Donissan".

Critics have long picked it out as a masterpiece, and even today it is acclaimed by retrospective admirers. The New Yorker recently wrote a piece on the film as part of their feature highlighting the finest pictures ever made. They lamented its absence from the US DVD market, writing "Its rarity is surprising, given that its star is Gérard Depardieu, who gives one of his greatest performances. Under the Sun of Satan is an extraordinary film, a religious drama with a carnal ferocity."

In 2010 The Guardian selected it for their classic DVD feature, writing that it featured "a performance of power and integrity from Depardieu as a self flagellating country priest." Another interesting retrospective piece was published on the Spirituality and Practice website, where they wrote, "This film graphically conveys the negative fallout from spiritual pride and boasts very strong performances by Gerard Depardieu as the religious zealot and Sandrine Bonnaire as the self-destructive sensualist. Although some have found this cinematic exploration of good and evil out of step with the times, others will see it as a credible reworking of an ancient and reputable religious theme."

Under the Sun of Satan is without humour of relief, is punishing and not a film you could describe as being enjoyable. But, of course, its aim is not to entertain but to provoke, to get one thinking about good, evil, God, the devil, faith, disillusionment, sin and temptation. It is a hugely rewarding experience, and though not easily accessible, an essential piece of masterful filmmaking.

A STRANGE PLACE TO MEET (1988)

A Strange Place to Meet, known in France as Drole d'endroit pour une rencontre, is one of those rare gems that, for one reason or another, has unfortunately disappeared into obscurity. Directed by Francois Dupeyron, from a script co written with Dominique Faysse, it's a beautifully acted drama of unfulfilled desire and indifference.

The plot, or the outline at least, concerns Catherine Deneuve (seemingly more beautiful as she got into her forties) having an argument with her husband - or as we are told - while he is driving them down a frantic highway. When he nearly runs over a mad woman who rushes into the middle of the road, he swerves the car off to one side, stops and ends up throwing Deneuve out into the night, leaving her there and driving off into the darkness. At the road side is Gerard Depardieu, a surgeon having some car trouble, claiming he has been there for to days trying to fix the engine. At first irritated by Deneuve's presence, given she insists on waiting there for the husband she insists will return to pick her up, he develops a strange infatuation for her, masochistically pushing her away through the night, alienating her, and then trying to win her over. She sleeps in Depardieu's car and wakes in the morning to frantically ask the other sleeping drivers in the lay-by if they have seen her husband. They answer no, but undeterred by the rejection, she refuses to leave and insists he will come back for her.

Eventually Depardieu convinces her to come with him to a nearby cafe, where he hilariously fusses over choosing the right table where they can have their morning coffee and sandwiches. Tensions develop, with Depardieu clearly developing a crush on, if not an obsession with this strange woman who would wait a year for a man never intending to return. She on the other hand, could not care less for Depardieu as a possible romantic distraction, irritated by his heavy handedness and ineptness with women. They stay at the cafe another full day and night, coming across all types of people; these include a woman who agrees to sell Deneuve the outfit she is wearing, because it reminds her of one she used to wear for her husband in happier times; and a group of crude, hard drinking truckers, one of whom spends the night with Deneuve, pulling the curtains closed on the window to his truck as Depardieu, sitting across in his car, reacts with the extreme jealousy of a bitter husband. What will become of Deneuve and Depardieu, the obsessed and the object of the obsession?

A Strange Place to Meet is a play put to film, a series of unfolding events which border on the surreal, the absurd, and are often plain funny and strangely farcical. Depardieu puts in a complex, multi faceted performance as a man in love but also a slave to his own uselessness with the fairer sex. Deneuve is magnificent, striking as ever of course, but portraying a muddled, confused, put upon, if not totally mad woman. There is an air of mystery about her, with certain behavioural traits suggesting the husband is not a husband at all, maybe a boyfriend, perhaps something else. Some have even said she may be a lady of the night, one in the throes of madness, lamenting a husband that does not even exist. Either way, whether a crazed enigma or unhappy wife, slowly being dropped on to the rubbish heap, Depardieu is besotted, yet tortured by her disinterest.

The most interesting dynamic here, between two of French cinema's brightest lights, is the fact that Deneuve is desperate for love and acceptance, but attempting to earn it from a man who couldn't care less. Perversely, Depardieu is the same, hungry if not starving for Deneuve's love, but getting shunned heartlessly. Neither can see the truth before them, blinded as they are by their ignorance and love induced madness; Deneuve with a man who would drop everything for her, Depardieu faced with a woman denying him every step of the way.

Curiously, Dupeyron does not make this a beautiful film. Even though I viewed an old VHS, it was clear to me that Dupeyron was not concerned with aesthetics, but tension, atmosphere and a certain raw reality. The camera stays on the characters in long takes, angles are straight forward, never fussy, and emphasis at all times is on man and woman; Deneuve and Depardieu, the spaces between them, the gaps which cannot be filled. The only real artful shot, repeated a few times through the long nights, is of a wispy mist drifting silently over the moon. This is a film to watch for the performances, and thankfully the director takes a step back and allows the two legends to do their work. They are marvellous from beginning to end.

It was greeted warmly upon release and is regarded highly by those in the know. Tine Out wrote: "Talk about minimal: Dupeyron's feature debut is a road movie where they only travel 10 kilometres. Deneuve's in the throes of a very heavy, possibly masochistic relationship with the man who dumped her; Depardieu is a lonely, romantic doctor who's doggedly hopeless with the opposite sex. Nothing is entirely resolved, tempting hints about the characters' lives aren't elaborated upon (*is* she married, mad, or a high class hooker?), and the film retains the haunting inconsequentiality of a chance encounter. The romantic protestations, set against the grim background of a plastic café, are poignant and dreamlike, the characters are drifters seeking refuge or escape, and the whole film is comic and bitter-sweet."

The New York Times however found it frustrating, perhaps confused by the lack of explanations and solutions, with Janet Maslin writing the following: "For neophyte acting students, this material might seem worth playing to the hilt, but for two of the French cinema's greatest stars it's an odd choice indeed. The reasons why Mr. Depardieu and Miss Deneuve chose to co-produce A Strange Place to Meet will be, for anyone who sees the film, a complete mystery. Among the more absurd touches here, beyond the sight of Miss Deneuve wandering dazedly around a truck stop in her dark glasses and sable, are the fact that Mr. Depardieu is supposed to be a surgeon and the peculiar identification that Miss Deneuve's character feels with a woman who has, at the beginning of the story, tried to jump in front of her car."

For me, the fact that Depardieu and Deneuve chose this abstract material proved they were happy to take risks, to go against the star system and choices expected of them. Admirers of the two leads will find A Strange Place to Meet an absolute delight, a film not afraid to go off track, dwell on minor details and go on side tangents. Refreshingly ragged in style, the lack of technique and reliance on frilly camera work makes more room for these two towering talents, playing the kind of characters you might meet in a strange dream, rather than on the big screen.

CAMILLE CLAUDEL (1988)

As the 1980s went on, Gerard Depardieu continued to give staggeringly good performances in a series of formidable films. Indeed, his run of excellence in this decade put other actors to shame - not that Depardieu was in the acting game to compete of course. But looking at the progress he made from his streetwise roughneck persona of the 1970s - fighting and screwing his way through Going Places, chopping off his penis as the ape man of The Last Woman and so on - and it's astonishing to think that within the next few years he would be portraying such complex parts as Martin Guerre, the hunchback in Jean de Florette, the tortured priest in Under the Sun of Satan, and then, here, the sculptor Rodin in the intense and compelling Camille Claudel.

The brilliant Isabelle Adjani plays Camille Claudel, a young woman starting her sculpting career in 1880s Paris, who begins an affair with Auguste Rodin, played by Depardieu. The film establishes Camille's character and her early days working with Rodin, building towards their affair and the intensity of their relationship. When other factors enter their lives however, it seems that Camille and Auguste's union might not be strong enough to survive Rodin's incredible fame and his dalliances with another woman.

Camille Claudel was based on the book by Camille's brother Paul, whose memories of the affair were thankfully put down in print. Directed by Bruno Nuytten, he also co wrote the script with Marilyn Goldin. Having worked as a cameraman on many key films of the period (not to mention Going Places and Borocco), this was his first outing as director. He guides the film with an unshowiness, but captures the vital emotion on display, the tension, while also setting each scene out with expertise and making sure the viewer never forgets what era they are watching, without detracting from the story of course.

It is, however, a film to watch for the performances, which it has to be said, are of the highest quality. Adjani is a revelation here. She had of course been great on screen before this (one thinks of Borocco with Depardieu, The Story of Adele H, or as the tormented lady in Werner Herzog's remake of Nosferatu), but this feat just has to be the finest moment of her career. Nominated for an Oscar for her work, the film brought her international acclaim, as well as a Silver Bear award and a Cesar for Best Actress.

Depardieu puts in a fine and controlled performance as Rodin, clearly a world away from the early thug parts he played. His versatility was now at its peak, and the man was seemingly able to take on any role he pleased. His power here is something to behold, from the way he storms into a room to the manner in which he harshly moves around his models as if they were lumps of clay, objects without feeling there to solely inspire him. The chemistry between Gerard and Isabelle is also rather special, their passion burning off the screen and only occasionally spilling over into the overly melodramatic. When they first meet she insists she is underwhelmed, but the atmosphere between them quickly changes. It seems to begin in one key scene, when they both revolve a naked woman modelling for him in his studio, and there is clearly an intense like-mindedness. From then on, there is only one way for the pair to go.

The film was very successful, both at the world box office and with critics. It won the Best Film gong at the Cesars and received a nomination for Best Foreign Language Film at the Oscars. A massive success in France, it arrived in America heavily applauded. Yet some of the American reviews were rather odd. The New York TImes said that Depardieu's presence made it one of the best "bad" movies ever made. While finding it over the top, they applauded Depardieu's work: "Mr. Depardieu, though not on the screen throughout, makes an arresting Rodin, whether or not he bears much resemblance to the man he portrays. Only an actor of his heft and presence could play such a subsidiary role without being overwhelmed by his co-star. His Rodin is a funny, arrogant, passionate man, whose refusal to leave his aging common-law wife (Daniele Lebrun) for the younger Camille somehow seems perfectly understandable under the circumstances."

Roger Ebert however plainly loved it, writing of Gerard, "Depardieu plays a Rodin who is genial, assured and malevolent. He will go only so far for a woman before he must pull back and be sure that his ego is served. Has there ever been another actor, in any language, who seems so unselfconsciously assured in such a variety of roles? Depardieu works all the time, always well, and just within the last few years he has been not only Rodin but also the hunchback peasant of Jean de Florette and the love-struck car salesman of Too Beautiful for You."

Writing retrospectively, James Travers on the French Films website called it a "flawed masterpiece", adding that the performances were respectable rather than great. Agreed, the picture is slow moving at times, and perhaps a little over long, but it is gripping too. Camille Claudel also has a strained mood to it, making the viewer uneasy at all times, because we aware that something bad is looming around the corner. This is no typical period piece, nor is it a film about Camille's art, so often overlooked; it is about her passions, her need to sculpt, but also her need for Rodin, conflicting with her desire to exist outside his shadow as a woman in her own right.

Depardieu on the cover of Premiere in 1989

TROP BELLE POUR TOI (1989)

Gerard Depardieu was back with Bertrand Blier once more with Trop Belle Pour Toi, known in English as Too Beautiful For You. Closer to the work of Jean Luc Godard than their previous work together, Too Beautiful For You constantly plays with logic, ones idea of what makes sense and what doesn't. This provocative, confrontational and darkly funny film more than measures up to the likes of Going Places, Buffet Froud and Get Out Your Handkerchiefs, even if there is a shift in style.

It stars Depardieu as Barthelemy Bernard, a BMW dealership owner who seems to have it all; good job, plenty of money, status, lots of friends, a child, a beautiful home and an equally beautiful wife, played by the striking Carole Bouquet. Tipping everything upside down early on in the film, Gerard's character falls for Colette (Josiane Balasko), a plain and seemingly ordinary secretary he has recently hired. She does not have the beauty of his wife, but then she doesn't have her shortcomings either, her delusions and pretences. As their affair continues, Barthelemy sees his life change beyond recognition; all the while the music of Schubert plays loudly, not always in the background, but often interfering with and even dominating whole scenes.

Too Beautiful For You is not an instantly "easy" film to watch, but then if you are up for a challenge it is worth sticking with and getting used to. In fact, its unconventional qualities end up enriching it, lifting it from more straight forward and predictable romantic dramas. While this kind of tale would normally involve a middle aged man cheating on his dour wife with a beauty, immediately Blier decides to invert expectations and lampoon the popular cliché, indeed as he had in Buffet Froid and Get Out Your Handkerchiefs. Rich in visuals and ideas, it is also ironic, self aware (in a good way) and mischievous, being full of typical Blier humour. It also shares something with Get Out Your Handkerchiefs; an obsession with music from a single composer, with the earlier Mozart here being replaced by the more intrusive and often irritating Schubert. While characters are forced to shout over the music in certain scenes where someone is playing Schubert a little too loudly, Depardieu himself is driven to near insanity by it, to the point that at the very end he shouts to the camera how much Schubert has been winding him up for the previous 90 minutes. He breaks down the fourth wall, merely to align himself with our own belief that movie soundtracks can manipulate and often ruin the direction of a film. Paradoxically, by highlighting this flaw in popular movies, Blier creates something unique, where his main character has become aware of the soundtrack.

Blier's film is not merely a repeat of themes and concepts from earlier work, but a totally fresh and individual film in its own right. Characters speak to camera, openly express frustration and thoughts usually limited to the inner mind, and in other scenes they appear in flashback within the new scene, so that past and present overlap and cohabitant time. Rather than setting up a straight forward narrative, Blier establishes his unique approach to this meditation on love and relationships, not to mention the enigma of desire itself, with striking images which highlight Depardieu's new found passion in contrast to what he has at home. As beautiful as his wife may be, he is also bored by her confidence, her self assuredness and control over those around her. One scene early on is key; it involves the couple having dinner with friends, she holding court with a pretentious monologue which, though enrapturing the others, leaves Depardieu cold. "Is there a point to this?" he asks. Right away, he is refreshed by the plain secretary's openness, her straight forward air and the other qualities which the more beautiful naturally do not possess. This is a film of infatuation, about the mystery of attraction. Right away, we wonder what Depardieu sees in her which he doesn't have at home. Half way through we understand it more, but at the end we are just as confused and conflicted as he is.

Blier's film was very acclaimed upon release. It also swept the Cesar Awards, winning Best Film, Best Writing, Best Directing, Best Editing and Best Director for Carole Bouquet, as well as the Special Prize at Cannes Film Festival. Elsewhere the film was held up as a masterpiece. John Mount wrote of the film for Empire: "Bertrand Blier, who has always tried to provide something to offend everyone in his surreal, black comedies, delivers his finest outing in years in this parable on the dangers of confusing your stereotypes and taking a mistress as a wife and vice versa. Depardieu has a field day as the wandering husband, torn between two women for all the wrong reasons and crumbling into indecision with cruel, ironic results. All very French, of course, and although the mordant humour and various outrageous twists look in danger of unravelling at the end, Depardieu's indiscretion finally comes home to roost with a satisfying vengeance. Social observation with a sledgehammer."

Roger Ebert, though admitting it was a challenge, was impressed with Blier's commitment, writing "This is grown up love, not the silly adolescent posturing of Hollywood sex symbols. It is love beyond sex, beyond attraction, beyond lust. It is the love of need..." On Depardieu, firstly describing him as a man who looks scared that he is always about to break something, he wrote, "(he) is one of the most endlessly fascinating actors of our time. He works constantly, in roles of such variety that to list them is astonishing. Here he plays an ordinary man, one of the most difficult roles in the movies. He makes his passion believable because he never over acts it."

Indeed, this is a tricky role for him, but Depardieu pulls it off wonderfully, never over cooks the part, nor makes anything seem unbelievable in this purely surreal film, one which no doubt Breton himself would have approved of. He is natural in a film that is anything but, and that in itself makes this performance a tour de force and among his finest portrayals of the everyman faced with a challenging predicament.

Too Beautiful For You is perhaps the finest study of that phenomenon known as amour fou, and is certainly among Blier's most satisfying films.

GREEN CARD (1990)

For those unfamiliar with French cinema, and therefore Depardieu's own legacy within its rich history, Green Card might just be the most prominent image they have of Gerard Depardieu. He had been making films in France for over twenty years at this point, and though some of his pictures had been successful overseas, either at art house cinemas or within the critics' circles, his work was little known to most UK and US filmgoers, even if his face and name were familiar. In truth he was one of the world's most popular and recognisable actors, which is curious given the fact that many English speaking people might have had only a vague idea of his filmography. Green Card then, if nothing else, was going to give them the opportunity to experience the undeniable charm and charisma of Monsieur Depardieu. Thankfully, as the film was so effectively executed, it gave them much more than a mere starring vehicle for France's premier star. Thirty years on, it is still a very funny, hugely enjoyable and lovably sweet movie.

Andie MacDowell plays Bronte (her father named all his children after famous writers), a horticulturist who agrees to marry a Frenchman named George Faure (Depardieu) so he can get his green card to work and live legally in America, and she can rent a beautiful apartment adorned with tropical plants which only lets in married couples. They meet in the Afrika Cafe, are married, shake hands and assume they will never see each other again. When the Immigration office gets in touch however, Georges must visit Bronte's house to undergo an interview. Concocting stories that they met while both holding parcels, and that he has been away in Africa (the country, not the cafe they agree to meet in), the pair try to convince the investigators they are a couple in love. When Georges' behaviour rouses suspicion, a more thorough interview is set up for a Monday morning. Reluctantly upon the advice of her lawyer, she agrees to let Georges move in for a couple of days so they can learn more about one another and convince at the impending interrogation. While forced together, Georges irritates Bronte but also charms her. They are total opposites in many ways (she is a health fanatic, he a devourer of life unconcerned with trivial matters like dieting), but she is won over by his care-free attitude. Despite frictions, they begin to fall for one another, but their fate lies in how well they fare against the Immigration Office.

Peter Weir, already a director of note with a series of notable pictures behind him, wrote Green Card with Depardieu in mind. Clearly a big fan of his work, he wished to introduce the star to US audiences. With the script written, Weir learned that, though Gerard was up for a collaboration, he was fully booked with back to back film work for the next year. "That was a tremendous disappointment," Weir told Premiere Magazine in 1990, "because we had met, ideas were flowing, and I sensed that it would be a very good collaboration. But, of course, I was quite happy to wait. I mean, what else could I do?" While waiting for Depardieu's hectic schedule to clear, he went and directed Dead Poet's Society... not a bad way to pass the time in retrospect.

When Weir spoke to Cinema Papers in 1990, he expressed his admiration for Depardieu: "It's an original screenplay by me for Gerard Depardieu. A number of the character details are actually taken from his life. I admire him, and it seems an awful loss that he is largely unknown to English-speaking audiences, apart from real filmgoers. Most people just don't go to foreign movies. Gerard is approaching 40 and I wanted to bring him something he could do in English. So, I tailored it. I knew he spoke English, though not fluently, and I tried to combine those elements of talents that I'd seen on screen in various French movies - from the comedic sense to his edge of mystery, his romantic side. He likes to work with *auteurs*, with writer-directors, and be part of the process of developing the screenplay. He doesn't just take a job; he likes to have a complete involvement. He's not interested in just turning up and being paid. He would never go to Hollywood and make a James Bond film. Gerard came to Sydney for a couple of weeks last November so that we could work together."

Some insiders at the time claimed Depardieu took on the film because he wished to be a star in America. The most French of actors, he was content with his life as France's Number One actor, though admittedly he did perhaps dream of American big screen fame. He did Green Card for the script, and though he has appeared in Hollywood films since, he is never totally comfortable in American pictures. "I am not so hungry to be a movie star," he said upon the release of Green Card. "I don't care about that, I really don't. When Peter gives me the first script, I saw one thing for me - the story of a man and woman who have to invent in 48 hours a life. For me, this is a great situation, because you can make a comedy with that, but you can also make the truth."

Depardieu and Weir got along famously while making Green Card. An on set report ran: "Depardieu and Weir, who have grown as close brothers, are a study in contrasts. Depardieu is smoking Gitanes, wearing black from head to foot, yakking away in his disarmingly fractured English. Weir's brand loyalty is to Marlboro, high-top sneakers are his only concession to black, and his French is fluent."

"He's this unique collaborator," Weir said on set, "in that he really draws your creation out of you and inspires you to go further with it. In a sense, he becomes you. I think that probably only happens when something is written for him, as Blier and Pialat have done. He sort of burrows his way into your character's life."

MacDowell herself later admitted she was initially intimidated by the idea of working with European cinema's most dangerous and wild performer. "He has such an ease with himself that he just makes you feel comfortable." And comfortable is the key word to the charm and chemistry between MacDowell and Depardieu. The script is brilliant of course and Weir steers clear of the usual Hollywood clichés, but the film succeeds because the stars are believable, natural, and though their falling in love might seem unlikely on paper (and a familiar film plot twist), Gerard and Andie give it something special with their authenticity. Indeed, one believes they really have fallen for each other, but more organically, less dramatically than they might have in a lesser Hollywood picture.

Of course, it helps that Green Card was not a conventional Hollywood production, an independent film which, in Weir's own words, was "an auteur film, made overseas by an Australian director with the involvement of French components." It is brilliantly filmed and directed with an ease which makes it seem as if it was effortlessly assembled, itself a skill hard to pull off. The supporting cast are brilliant, Bebe Neuwirth in particular as Bronte's friend, but the picture belongs to the wonderful duo of MacDowell and Depardieu. In many ways, Green Card is the perfect doorway for the Gerard newcomer, an ideal way to enter his rich and rewarding filmography. It is also one of his easiest, most pleasant and approachable films, an accessible romantic comedy without the surrealistic edge of his work with Blier, or the danger of the characters he played in such films as Loulou, Maitresse and Buffet Froid. To think that this is even the same actor is a testament to Depardieu's staggering range. Though still a man with a rough past (he undoubtedly draws on autobiographical details in the role, such as the allusions to a criminal past and leaving home at 12), he is at his most open and charming here.

Depardieu rightly won a Best Actor award at the Golden Globes, though the film itself was met with mixed reviews. Most however, agreed that both stars were excellent. "Mr. Depardieu, in the role that gets him into a New York Yankees cap," wrote the New York Times, "proves that he is nothing if not a sport... He comes to life most fully when he lapses into French or is otherwise momentarily freed from the story's constraints." Roger Ebert, a long time admirer of Depardieu, was under no impression that the film was a classic, but he did write a favourable review: "It is not blindingly brilliant, and is not an example of the very best work of the director who made The Year of Living Dangerously or the actor who starred in Cyrano de Bergerac. But it is a sound, entertaining work of craftsmanship, a love story between two people whose meeting is not as cute as it might have been."

It is odd to read retrospective reviews which compare Depardieu's work to more straightforward Hollywood fare, especially to someone more familiar with his work for Blier, Truffaut and company. Empire hilariously dubbed it "better than Ghost but not as good as When Harry Met Sally," but also made a valid point about the romance, stating "it's abundantly clear that the ox-like free spirit that is Georges would be bored silly with the precious Bronte. In fact, he would be far more likely to go for the charms of her best friend, Lauren (Neuwirth, familiar from TV's Cheers), at whose mother's snobby dinner party quite the best scene in the movie erupts as Depardieu reveals a hitherto little-recognised if idiosyncratic talent for music."

Green Card is a perfect film for those who grew up in the 1990s and are feeling a bit nostalgic, and for genuine fans of romantic comedies too. Depardieu admirers have to admit that, though it lacks the drive of the game changing likes of Buffet Froid, the depth of films like Jean de Florette and The Return of Martin Guerre, not to mention the bold power of Camille Claudel, it does feature some of the most memorable moments from his career; the scene where he tries to lead the immigration officer to the bathroom in an apartment he has never been in before; or the piano scene where he stuns the party guests with an impromptu piece of avant-garde improvisation, then a carefully played ballad over which he recites pained poetry. Green Card is a minor gem from the golden era of rom-coms.

Cyrano De Bergerac (1990)

CYRANO DE BERGERAC (1990)

The same year he embarked upon his first American adventure in Peter Weir's wonderful rom-rom Green Card, Gerard Depardieu took on a role that would become one of his most celebrated and acclaimed, that of Cyrano de Bergerac. Directed by Jean Paul Rappeneau and adapted from Edmond Rostand's immortal play, it is a classic, iconic story for the ages, one which no matter how many times it is reworked and re-imagined never loses its poetic beauty. Though many might have singled out the 1950 version starring Jose Ferrer, Depardieu's tour de force has now become the essential interpretation of the romantic, chivalrous, long nosed hero.

Depardieu embodies Cyrano in a manner which suggests he was born to play him. This flamboyant poet is a swashbuckler, a cad, a man who hides his insecurities, in particular those about his prominent nose, behind a jocular persona. Beneath his larger than life grandeur, Cyrano is hopelessly in love with his cousin Roxanne, played by Anne Brochet. Though outwardly confident, Cyrano is too afraid to declare his love, fearing her rejection and the fact she may find him physically repulsive. Roxanne falls for Christian (VIncent Perez), a handsome soldier who joins Cyrano's military unit. Though good looking, he finds it hard to communicate with women and is hardly a man of words. Seeing a chance to express his passion for Roxanne, the gifted Cyrano offers to assist Christian in wooing Roxanne, writing awe inspiring love poems which she assumes were written by Christian. Cyrano becomes frustrated when Roxanne falls completely in love and the pair get married. Will Roxanne ever learn the truth about Cyrano and the letters credited to Christian?

There really is no getting round the fact that Cyrano de Bergerac is a masterpiece, undeniably so, and is in fact one of the finest films in the history of French cinema. It is a tour de force in every area, from

Rappeneau's sweeping direction and the rich script, to Jean Claude Petit's wonderful score and Pierre Lhomme's bold cinematography. In the acting however, it must be said, the film rises to a whole different level of quality. All the performances are sublime, from Perez's dashing hero to Brochet's passionate Roxanne. The finest work here though, of course, is from Depardieu, who is a total revelation as Cyrano. From his first appearance in the film, when he rises from the back of the theatre to rouse up trouble, starting a wild and exuberant sword fight with a rival, he is charisma through and through, a force to be reckoned with and a truly formidable character. In classic Depardieu fashion though, he gives the part real depth, a duality which is poignant to say the least. Cyrano is a cartoonish role now because it is one so familiar to us all, but Gerard is too gifted an actor to lean on broad tactics. Beneath his act, his enviable wit and vibrancy, is a deeply insecure soul, embarrassed about the physical defect he mocks and belittles in his humorous monologues. One of Gerard's skills has always been in combining bold exteriors with sensitivity, and here it hits a kind of peak. This is the sort of role he might not have imagined he could have played, especially in the mid to late 70s when he was still in the midst of his angry male era, but he pulls it off to such an extent that it is literally impossible to imagine anyone else in the costume. A staggering feat, it remains perhaps his most everlasting piece of work and is likely to go down as his most celebrated performance.

Both the film and Depardieu received a great deal of acclaim, with Depardieu himself bagging a Cesar for Best Actor (his second, after The Last Metro), a Cannes Best Actor prize, and nominations at the Golden Globes and Academy Awards. Roger Ebert, in his review of the film, wrote of Depardieu, "his physical presence makes a definite statement on the screen, and then his acting genius goes to work, and transforms him into whatever is required for the role - into a spiritual priest, a hunchback peasant, a medieval warrior, a car salesman, a businessman, a sculptor, a gangster. Cyrano de Bergerac is a splendid movie... He plays Cyrano on the level, for keeps."

In the UK, Empire gave it 5 stars, writing "For all its spectacle and splendid all-round performances, however, Cyrano De Bergerac is without doubt Gérard Depardieu's film. His is the gentle giant, at times a spellbinding entertainer juggling words and his sword with equal ease, at others, a vulnerable, tongue-tied romantic in Roxane's presence. This is a moving performance which puts the heart firmly back into romance and surely guarantees much hanky-wringing in the aisles. Truly the Greatest Love Story Ever Told."

It seems that everybody agreed the film was a success and that Depardieu had reached a totally new level of performance. Even today it remains a classic. In February of 2020, the Times wrote "This was the turn that made Gérard Depardieu an international star, winning him the best actor award at Cannes and an Oscar nomination. He channels his ungainly charisma and mastery of pathos into the role of the poet/swashbuckler."

Speaking almost thirty years after making the film, Jean Paul Rappeneau recalled the shoot: "It was as if he had been touched by an angel's wing. There was a special atmosphere. When I think of Cyrano, I have zero regrets. I can't see who could possibly be better than Depardieu... That was my greatest success... thanks to Depardieu, thanks to many things." On Gerard himself, Rappeneau said, "He didn't know the play and he recognised himself in the story of a man who was at once very strong, capable of fighting a hundred people, and very weak, crippled by a secret wound that stops him loving anyone. There are 1500 Alexandrines to say in the play and Depardieu knew them all by heart. Ten years later he still remembered them. Perhaps it marked an end point for him. Today it bugs him to have to learn even short dialogues."

For an actor who relies on spontaneous magic, and the wonder of the moment as it happens, to be so enraptured by dialogue and the inner workings of a single character suggests that Depardieu related very much to Cyrano. The role most definitely stuck with him, and in various interviews, not to mention through the book Innocent, he frequently quotes Cyrano. That tenderness, vulnerability even, coupled with the brutish surface, the bravado that goes with a man performing to conceal insecurities, obviously spoke to Gerard.

On not winning the Oscar, Depardieu told Film Comment that he was "disappointed. Of course. But Cyrano couldn't be a less American character. American characters are very proud. Cyrano was very ambiguous, because he hates himself so much." Depardieu makes an interesting point, that overly confident people may fail to see the wonder of Cyrano, but anyone with depth will surely relate to a man who contains such contrasting if not paradoxical traits.

Speaking to Jean Pierre Lavoigant, Depardieu went into further detail about Cyrano, and how it was his destiny to play the man. "I get the impression that I've been preparing for it for twenty years. In the end, it was truly something that was inside of me every day. In terms of desire and of this communication. And I think that it's the most beautiful synthesis of communication, Cyrano I mean. It's the love that we all have inside of us, that comes out or doesn't come out, I mean, that exists, that is there, you know. It was magnificent to have done it like that at this age, at this turning point, with the energy that we had around us."

Of all his films, Cyrano de Bergerac is definitely up there with the best; in terms of complete rounded performances, it is perhaps his finest hour, a starting point for anyone aware of Depardieu's myth (after all, his name and reputation precedes him) but new to the magic and wonder he can ignite on the screen.

TOUS LES MATINS DU MONDE (1991)

Often seen as one of the seminal French films of the 1990s, Tous Les Matins du Monde won seven awards at that year's Cesars, including Best Film, Best Director for Alain Corneau and Best Supporting Actress for Anne Brochet. Depardieu was nominated for Best Actor, though sadly did not win. Still, it is essential Depardieu and should be included in anyone's list of his most important works.

The film itself, based on the book of the same title, focuses on Marin Marais, an ageing musician played by Gerard Depardieu who narrates the tale of his early life. In his younger years he is played by Gerard's son Guillaume Depardieu, when a student under his mentor, Monsieur de Sainte-Colombe. The film features the haunting viol of Jordi Savall, which does much to establish the melancholic atmosphere of the film and Marais' recollections.

Though at this stage it becomes vaguely embarrassing for other actors, especially anyone ever put up as a serious contender for Depardieu in this era, the great man gives another towering, formidable effort. It's a complete performance, measured and carefully played in every respect. Though I personally believe Depardieu has rarely given a bad performance (102 Dalmatians is up there though), his work here has to be seen and heard to be believed. There is poignancy in his recollections, the cob webbed relic in awe at his own talent when he was a youth, but Depardieu and indeed Corneau himself avoid all clichés and tempting pitfalls of familiarity. His lost love for Madeleine (Anne Brochet) is similarly low key and is never played for schmaltz's sake.

A critical and box office success, it was seen as one of the best films of the year by some. Roger Ebert gave it 3 out of 4 when it was released in America, writing "This is a simple story, made of three things: music, love, and regret." In the UK, Empire Magazine called it slow and

111

languorous, but also an "exquisite treat. Inevitably it's Depardieu Snr. who faultlessly carries us in the palm of his hand through the deeper lakes of longing and ennui, with his tear-stained Rembrandt of a face succeeding in summarising the story to a fine nuance."

The Los Angeles Times praised Corneau's film, writing of Gerard: "Depardieu, a great and indefatigable actor, starts the movie with a showstopper: a six-minute unbroken close-up in which the elderly Marais, in the last stages of his court career, reminisces brokenly on his relationship with the long-dead St. Colombe. His wig askew, his face a trembling ruin of tears, flabby cheeks and smeared rouge, Depardieu does a mesmerizing portrait of guilt, decay and vulnerability. When the film later moves into a sustained tone of sombre austerity, interrupted by violence, that first scene echoes over everything."

Though it seems impossible given what he had done before this, Depardieu seemed to mature and grow as an actor in the late 80s and early 90s. Some feel he hit a peak in this era, making few films deserving of his talents hereafter, but nonetheless Depardieu remained a formidable presence. Though he has delivered powerful performances since, his efforts here are nothing short of awe inspiring. As a side note, UK fans can get this as a part of the 4 DVD Depardieu set, alongside the French version of My Father the Hero, Buffet Froid and Colonel Chabert.

MON PERE, CE HEROS (1991)

One of Depardieu's lighter and more accessible French films is Mon Pere Ce Heros, known in English (and indeed remade, somewhat disappointingly, in America) as My Father the Hero. Written and directed by Gerard Lauzier, it stars Depardieu as Andre, a divorced father who, having worked and saved up to do so, takes his daughter Veronique (Marie Gillain) on holiday to an exotic island. The only problem is she is 14 going on 21, and much to Andre's dismay she is growing up too fast before his eyes. When she meets a local teenager, she concocts tales that Andre is actually her possessive lover, a secret agent who has had all kinds of adventures all over the world and takes her with him as his underage companion. While the false stories make their way around the hotel, Andre becomes confused and troubled by the funny looks he is getting. When his daughter tells him what has happened, he is at first outraged, then weirdly agrees to go along with her lies to impress the boy she wishes to woo. In the end, thankfully, the truth comes out and father and daughter reach a kind of understanding.

Mon Pere Ce Heros was a success upon release, even though some critics thought it muddled. Depardieu provides a funny, warm and appealing performance as a genuinely likeable and decent dad, a man who can see his daughter growing up, leaving the nest and drifting away from his paternal rule. Though at first he is saddened, threatened even, by her approaching adulthood, in the end he reaches an acceptance with a father's fate and his little girl. It's a touching finale to a film which runs at a continuously healthy pace and contains many memorable and funny moments.

Reviews were mixed though. Time Out were not impressed, writing in their review, "Proof positive that Depardieu is a star of international magnitude: even a pedestrian comedy like this warrants theatrical release in Britain. The picture lumbers from laborious farce to shameless sentiment with all the grace of a beached whale (an image Depardieu brings to mind). The bovine sensibility of this tacky, tasteless blague is underscored with misogyny and a scurrilous hint of racism."

UK's Empire were similarly disappointed, though they could not deny Depardieu put in a good effort: "Something of an unpalatable mix of The Blue Lagoon and Monsieur Hulot's Holiday, this syrupy teen romance would be all but unwatchable were it not for the presence of Depardieu, here lumbering through a slight plot... Indeed, it says much for Depardieu's professionalism that he emerges with his integrity virtually intact not only from a weak film but also a series of potentially humiliating sporting pursuits he takes up in an attempt to keep young Veronique occupied and out of reach of the red-blooded males cruising the island. More of Depardieu and less of Gillain's romantic trysts would have helped here, particularly as the film is strongest whenever he makes an appearance."

While I also did not find myself as involved in the daughter's shenanigans as I did with Depardieu's troubles (as a father myself, perhaps I related to the situation), in no way is the film as bad as critics have often made it out to be. Highly enjoyable, straight forward and charming, it's undeniably light Depardieu fare, but very welcome amidst the more subversive, unconventional, often challenging works that surround it in his filmography.

MERCI LA VIE (1991)

To claim one film by Bertrand Blier is more subversive, anarchic or funnier than any other may seem like doing the visionary himself a disservice (after all, all his films are brilliant), but though Merci La Vie is often seen as a minor entry in his filmography, to some a less focused, less satisfactory experience than his more celebrated work, in some ways it's his most liberated and therefore most liberating work. As it begins we assume - misguidedly maybe - that the film may follow a more or less cohesive narrative. Ten minutes in though, and one realises Merci La Vie is not concerned with a straight forward story line at all. As we know, Blier does not all together destroy the traditional film narrative, but redefines it, establishes the ensuing mood early on in a film so that the viewer therefore accepts whatever will come later on, no matter how ludicrous and surrealistic. In Merci La Vie he seems to go further than ever in destroying and then playfully reconstructing what a film is. It is both a cinema revolution in one sitting, and a celebration of all that is great and stupid about the movies. Of course, as always with Blier, it is about much more besides.

Charlotte Gainsbourg plays Camille, a teenager living in a quiet seaside town. One day, when at the beach pushing a trolley full of objects and oddly relaxed seagulls, she comes across Joelle (Anouk Grinberg), a young woman in a wedding dress who has just been beaten up and left by her boyfriend. Camille picks her up and puts her in the trolley, taking her home so she can recuperate. Pretty soon Joelle's wild side is revealed, and rather speedily the pair go out into the world to experience what life has to offer... and not all of it is good. Various characters come in and out of the plot, while the two girls find themselves in various eras, all indicated by a change in the colour of the lens. Among the supporting cast is Gerard Depardieu who plays Dr Worms, a medical researcher who has invented a sexually transmitted disease and infected Joelle with it so that he can be credited with finding its cure. And this, believe it or not, is one of the tamest parts of the film.

The whole thing is more of an experience than what we would usually call a film, a series of wonderfully directed vignettes connected by their absurdity. Though featuring its share of disturbing imagery, and scenes modern viewers might find offensive, it's miraculous that Blier's film is as funny as it is and remains a true comedy, albeit a post-modern one. What enriches Blier's parodying though is the fact that it lacks cynicism. Blier may be an intellectual, a critic of society and mankind, but he is not one jaded by humanity, or for that matter what is left of it. He remains curious about people, about human behaviour and failings, and is fearless when approaching isms and conflict. Some may read Merci La Vie as a meditation on feminism, or perhaps more to the point an unflinchingly brutal account of what the female has to put up with in society. It's all here, often in comic but sometimes blunt style; the abusive father, the beating husband, the intimidation of the male gaze. The two girls are at the centre of the film, though Anouk Ginberg's Joelle swings from strong modern woman to submissive old fashioned wife, one minute the manipulator of the male, the next the victim of his chauvinism. By going back and forth loosely and without constraints, Blier's surrealist style avoids preaching or side taking. It's simply presenting problems, and Merci La Vie has plenty of those to show off.

Indeed, there is much more explored here than male-female problems; let us not forget, that when the film first starts to go back in time at regular intervals, we are faced with the Nazis and their terrible regime. They first appear audibly only, the stomp of their boots through the French streets like a thunder storm about to cause serious bother. "Who are they?" someone asks. "The Germans," comes the reply, followed by an inquisitive, "Are they the ones who killed the Jews?" There are certainly some unsettling scenes involving the Nazis,

116

especially the scene when much of the cast are stripped nude, put in train bunkers and then machine gunned to the ground. But Blier immediately lets his main characters escape this hell. One of them reminds another that it's only a movie, while there is a wish to be in better films, "American films", and the suggestion that they go to Hollywood. They do end up there, but Jean Carmet, after reflecting on his career as a supporting actor, sits catatonic in his wheel chair while America's youth skateboards around him. It's the final shot of a film which brings together AIDS and the SS, causing one character to shout in frustration, "What era are we in now?"

This could be interpreted as cubist filmmaking, life seen from every angle, in every colour, every tinted tone, every viewpoint, every mood, even every time period. It's mind boggling for the first thirty minutes, but one quickly accepts and begins to be perversely addicted to Blier's blending of reality, fantasy, the current and the flashback, all with knowing touches of humour. When the film goes into a blue tinged sequence recalling past events, someone even asks, "Is this a flashback?" It's the ultimate de-construction of cinema. Some may have observed Blier's films becoming more fragmented through the 80s, moving from the anarchic non-logic of Going Places, Get Out Your Handkerchiefs and Buffet Froid, towards the more Godardian likes of Too Beautiful For You. While the latter film was focused on l'amour fou, highlighting Gerard Depardieu's character's predicament at having to choose between a beautiful wife and a dowdy but irresistible secretary, Merci La Vie sets itself much wider. After all, "life" is in the title, and Blier's view of existence is one of madness, chaos and dark beauty.

Merci La Vie was nominated for various Cesars, though was robbed of Best Film in my view. Reviews were good and the film did well across the world, mainly because Depardieu's fame was at its height in the wake of Green Card and Cyrano de Bergerac, two films which brought him a wider audience outside Europe. Time Out wrote "Is it all really happening, or just a movie, or simply Camille's dream? Snazzily shot, wittily performed and structured, Buñuel-fashion, according to the logic of a dream, this bizarre blend of road movie, comedy, psychodrama and various other genres shifts with wayward glee not only between times - the present (?) and WWII - but between colour, black-and-white and monochrome tints. Lending some coherence is a sense that every age has its crises (AIDS, the Holocaust), that life is shit; but Blier's precise intentions are finally unfathomable."

Empire Magazine, failing to see the point in coming up with a synopsis (wisely perhaps), liked the film, but were rather misguided in thinking that Blier's views were possibly the same as those held by his misogynist characters. "Whether the pair ultimately win over the excuses for manhood in this film or are merely rather gutsier victims than most, and whether the misogyny on display is Blier's or that of his characters is not entirely clear. Offensive it may be, but driven at a cracking pace - through image shifts from black-and-white to colour, through period changes from present day to the Occupation, and through cultural references from the war to AIDS - Merci La Vie is still an undeniably exciting, often funny, and thought-provoking ride."

In my opinion, Merci La Vie is one of the finest films ever to have come out of France and I believe it's a shame it isn't more widely appreciated as the game changer it should have been. Comparisons may be made to Bunuel and Godard, but Blier is his own man, a total artist in the truest sense, and totally individual. Merci La Vie, for anyone who has seen it, brings cinema up a level, into a totally different realm that makes one question the importance and value of narrative and clichéd plot developments. Is there a need for formula in art? Is there room for conventions and predictabilities? Not in the world of Bertrand Blier's tremendous Merci La Vie, that's for sure.

1492: CONQUEST OF PARADISE (1992)

After some success with his first American picture, Green Card (for which he deservedly won a Golden Globe) Gerard Depardieu signed up for a much bigger, though not necessarily better (as he would find out) venture, this one with superstar director Ridley Scott. From a script by Roselyne Bosch, 1492: Conquest of Paradise tells the story of Christopher Columbus, the legendary Italian explorer who discovers the New World. In a curious piece of casting, which actually works at the end of the day, Depardieu plays Columbus, though the film itself, largely fictionalised and often quite ludicrous, is undeserving of the fine effort Gerard puts into it.

Bosch's original aim in writing the film was apparently to "explore the most exciting theory about him - that he was a rebel who pushed the limits of his time. You can not imagine a more complex personality than this." Who better then, than Depardieu, the icon of French cinema, the man who combined vulnerability with raw power, to portray this most conflicting of men? Once Scott was on board as director, intrigued by Bosch's approach to the man, then came the decision to cast Gerard.

"I think that Columbus was an artist," Depardieu said, seeing much to admire in the iconic figure. "Because when a man is looking for paradise, he's also looking for harmony, willing to find a better world. And that is the idea of an artist. I identify with all characters who feel the need to see something new. For a man like Columbus, anything is possible." Without the mention of Columbus, Depardieu could have been speaking about himself, the French star who was going to Hollywood to live out a childhood dream, to be a star of the American big screen.

Unfortunately, despite giving a solid performance in a far from solid film, American mega stardom passed Depardieu by. At first it was said he was disappointed by the film's negative criticisms and modest box office, but in retrospect its lack of success meant that Depardieu returned to France, where he made his purest, most satisfying work for auteur directors in smaller films. Here though, he more than holds his own against the American cast, in fact carrying the picture with a bold effort that few actors of the era could have matched.

Depardieu was right to be disappointed with its reception. Some deemed it a turkey, while others saw much to admire. Long time Gerard admirer Roger Ebert liked aspects of the film, and thought Depardieu held it up. Despite criticisms, Ebert said "Still, in its own way and up to a certain point, 1492 is a satisfactory film. Depardieu lends it gravity, the supporting performances are convincing, the locations are realistic, and we are inspired to reflect that it did indeed take a certain nerve to sail off into nowhere just because an orange was round."

Empire gave it four out of five, writing "As for Gerard Depardieu, he's the stand-out - loping around like a particularly charismatic sore headed bear, and playing triumph, passion and crushing disappointment with equal Gallic aplomb."

Though some see cinema as a primarily visual medium, and indeed some of American cinema largely is just that (all surface), the best films Depardieu has made have been ones where understanding of the characters' internal struggles are paramount. He may not care much about the complexities of his characters' psychology, but there is no doubt that the gems he made for Godard, Blier and company relied on intellectualism and human nature more than mere visuals. Scott is very much a visual filmmaker, ever ready to present the image as all. Here, with 1492, he presents a handsome film, but Depardieu's deep, careful portrayal of this great man belongs in a different film.

HELAS POUR MOI (1993)

There's avant garde, and then there's Jean Luc Godard. One of the most revolutionary, influential and important filmmakers in the history of the medium, Godard's career is something of a mine field for the newcomer. And if you are unfamiliar with his work, then Helas pour moi, though an interesting and eventually rewarding watch, is certainly not the best place to start.

Anyone tuning into Helias pour moi and expecting a straight forward narrative, as indeed the back of the DVD cover seems to suggest it may contain, will be very surprised. Based as it is on the legend of Alcmene and Amphitryon, its basic premise is that of a God visiting earth to experience human feelings and desire. Bernard Verley plays Abraham Klimt, who arrives in a small Swiss town with a view of investigating what exactly happened on the fateful day of July 23, 1989. We learn from a photograph he observes in their work place that the people involved were Rachel and Simon Donnadieu (Laurence Masliah and Gerard Depardieu respectively). Klimt goes around town asking questions to anyone and everyone who might have information, including the staff of a video store, proudly displaying posters and VHS covers of the newest, most shallow movies. We see Simon and Rachel's tale in a disjointed flashback and observe a god coming to earth taking on the form of Simon Donnadieu himself (the real Simon has gone away for a while) in a hope to obtain Rachel. Do the God and Rachel really experience something together, or is it all a part of the myth?

It is worth knowing that Godard's original idea had been for the god to be riding a train across Europe, watching battles and mankind's struggles from his window. Given it required special effects, ones perhaps not within Godard's budget, the concept was scrapped and the idea of the Swiss village was then pursued. Who knows what kind of results the train idea might have produced? In its finished form

Godard's film is challenging to watch, even for some more familiar with his work. The fragmented story, the time setting overlapping without warning, plus voice over, captions and the creepy voice of the visitor croaking over the soundtrack, make for refreshingly difficult viewing. Yes, there is perverse enjoyment in such a trial.

By the early 90s when he shot Helas pour moi, Godard had been deconstructing and redefining film for decades, a leading light of the French New Wave responsible for genuine masterpieces like Breathless, A Married Woman, Alphaville and Week-end. As the 70s turned into the 80s, Godard seemed to become even more avant garde, still coming out with genuinely awe inspiring works like 1982's Passion, but also warping the expectations of film with his reworking of King Lear. By the 1990s, anyone unfamiliar with his earlier work might have felt like they were going insane watching one of his features, and Helas pour moi is one I can imagine causing serious head aches. It is a disorientating experience at times, but in the way it mixes myth, legend, reality, rumour and fantasy ensures it keeps you thinking long after it's over. The first viewing may feel as if you are being bombarded from every angle, but a second viewing, once aware what is actually happening, is much more fulfilling.

With all the overlapping of dialogue, shouting, quick cuts and often distracting title cards, there is a plot to follow which becomes clearer in the final 30 or so minutes. Godard cleverly never tells us if a divine act has really been performed, as the God will not admit to Simon if he did have an encounter with Rachel, and given all the gossiping of the town folk, it may all be an exaggerated anecdote. When Depardieu says that "All men are the shadow of God to the women who love them," it becomes clear that Simon and the God are one and the same, interchangeable, but also that man is not a God but an image of one. While some might have expected Godard to go for an anti religious film about the myth of faith over its reality, he relented from doing so. Godard does however allude to belief coming in the absence of logic.

Godard later spoke about the making of the film, and called it a flop. Knowing full well that it would not have been financed without Depardieu's name attached, he was irritated by the actor's apparent (in his view at least) lack of interest during filming, finding the collaboration disappointing. "It could have been a good movie," he said, "if Depardieu was willing to try. But he was not interested in the movie, in working to make it right. Of course he said, 'Godard is a genius.' He was just making it for my name." With this in mind, it's hard to grasp what exactly Godard thought Depardieu had done wrong in his competent performance.

No one has really got to the bottom of what Helas pou moi says, but it is perhaps a meditation on the human condition, or the potential holiness and purity of the carnal act, as if it is the closest man gets to divinity. With messages to one side, it's a perversely enjoyable head-musher, complete with beautiful cinematography by Champetier and some scenarios that are extremely memorable.

Helas pour moi actually attracted some positive reviews upon its release. And because of Depardieu's presence it actually made it out across seas for a wider release. Variety were confused though: "(It is) elegantly photographed and recorded but lacks the incisive wit and visual daring of Godard's pioneering early work. It won't win any new converts."

The Los Angeles Times were more open minded: "Jean-Luc Godard's Helas Pour Moi is beautiful, terse, perplexing, allusive as it is elusive-- and a stunning experience if you're prepared to bring to it near-total alertness and openness. It helps a lot if you're an admirer well versed in the films of the ever-evolving New Wave pioneer, one of the giants of the cinema."

Occasionally funny, always pleasant on the eye, if not consistently for the brain, Helas pour moi is not and will never be seen as one of Godard's finest works, but it is a worthwhile experience and should not be overlooked all together.

GERMINAL (1993)

Without doubt, Germinal is one of the most devastatingly powerful films I have ever seen. While a two and a half hour French film about the plight of 19th century miners might not be everyone's idea of fun, Germinal is undeniably a great film in the truest sense, as entertainment and food for thought. While raising serious concerns about slave labour, poverty and inequality within society, it has the bonus of not merely being a history lesson on the roots of socialism in France. Indeed, it is an intensely gripping and, despite the heavy subject matter, extremely engaging drama of human tragedy.

It is set in an 1800s French mining village, and focuses on the life of the miners. The story is seen through the eyes of the aspiring socialist radical Etienne, played by Renaud, who arrives in town and quickly finds himself working in the mine. As he sets out to work, he is taken under the wing of the loyal and warm hearted Toussaint Maheu (Gerard Depardieu), and becomes a kind of honorary family member, even moving into the spare bed when the eldest daughter marries and leaves home.

As the film goes on, and Renaud expresses his outrage at the vast difference between the hard work they put in and the meagre pay they get in return, he begins to instigate a revolution, suggesting a strike might be the best way to get some form of justice. The film often cuts across to the mine owner, a rich tycoon, who regularly enjoys rich and ostentatious banquets with relatives and friends. The boss is aware a strike is imminent but seems unwilling to bend. The feeling from the rich is that the workers should be grateful they have any food at all, not to mention running water, heating and a roof over their head. But all they are asking for is a little fairness, a bit of extra bread to feed the mouths of their children. As the privileged dine on extravagant feasts, they resent even tossing extra crumbs to the miners.

The film is compulsively watchable in its first hour, even when merely showing the day to day life of the miners, their coal covered faces, the post-dinner bath when returning home and the weekend parties that make life that little bit more bearable. It is when Etienne convinces the genial Depardieu to consider what can be achieved by a collective show of solidarity that the film shifts, changes gear and becomes a gruelling and often upsetting study of greed, honour, misguided action and stubborn integrity.

Germinal was based on the classic novel by Emile Zola, adapted to the screen by director Claude Berri with the assistance of Ariette Langmann. Even though the film is lengthy, it never feels so and the pace is healthy. Berri directs with a straight forward confidence, capturing the rigorous life style of the miners, constantly dirty, living in the darkness and returning home, starving and exhausted, for their buttered bread. Berri cleverly contrasts these scenes against the ones involving the rich, with everyone garishly lit and brightly decorated. Berri does not highlight the class difference for cheap effect, nor does he exploit the poor workers to make his point; he simply draws a parallel, relying on the politics of each viewer to reach their own conclusions about the social injustice. The scales are undoubtedly weighed down, disgustingly so in fact, but the miners and their families are relatively happy despite being little more than slave labourers.

Though the film provokes thought about what it is to work, and to slave for a man stuffing his own belly while you count the pennies to make ends meet, the real strength comes with the characters, who are superbly drawn out and played by the fine cast. Renaud is superb as our eyes through this illuminating journey, a decent man who wants justice for the people he has found himself rubbing shoulders with and genuinely caring about. His wide eyed idealism might be naive, but his motives are good and pure, if unrealistic. Him being at the centre of the tale is vital; when we first see the goings on down the mines, the conditions in which the miners must work, and then when we see them in their homes, we share his shock, surprise and disgust.

Depardieu is extremely likeable as the head of the Maheu family, a thoroughly decent and hard working man who Gerard embodies with a sense of respect. One feels Depardieu likes the man he is playing, and he ensures Maheu keeps his pride from beginning to end. Miou-Moiou, Gerard's co star twenty years earlier in Bertrand Blier's Going Places, is staggeringly good as his wife, the family rock in some ways, and a woman who stands by her husband and the rest of the miners when they strike, calling anyone who betrays their motives a scab. She is an honourable, strong woman too, clearly struggling day to day but never letting it get on top of her. "We didn't eat," she says at the end of the film, "but at least we were together." She gives a tremendous performance, combining genuine desperation with a mother's pride wonderfully. In fact the whole cast are brilliant, especially Judith Henry as Depardieu's daughter Catherine, who ends up working down the mine, harbouring feelings for Etienne the newcomer, but getting involved with the arrogant, drunken bore Chaval, played excellently by Jean Roger Milo.

Germinal trigger all kinds of thoughts and inner paradoxes as the film progresses. Given it was written by Zola, who penned the book after spending time in a rural mining town in 1884, the adapted film has a painfully evocative authentic air, so we smell the mud, feel the coal in our own chests and smell the stenches of the pit, the dirt and the sweat combined. Indeed, the detail is staggering. Its aesthetic qualities aside, the themes explored summarise what was wrong with the pre-union working environment, and while proposing options, the film highlights the problems that will inevitably arise when men do not see eye to eye, and when matters get out of hand. The idea of the strike itself makes sense, but once the strike turns to rioting, the destruction of property and pure anarchy, the strike begins to appear a primal and misguided act. It's clear on Depardieu's face in one moment when the strike gets out of hand that deep down he knows the whole thing might be a mistake and no change will come of it. One scene in particular, the most shocking in t he film, shows how mob rule can lead to mayhem. When the protesters scare a bread seller out of his shop, he takes to the roof in fear. After he slips and falls to his death, dirt is shoved in his dead mouth, and one enraged wife (one the bread seller earlier deemed too ugly to have sex with) takes a knife and slices off his penis, holding it in the air like a trophy of victory. "Throw it to the dogs," shouts one miner. The look on Depardieu's face says it all. He is afraid of what the situation has become and what the consequences may be. He need not say a word, it's in the eyes.

Yet no one can argue with the fact that the workers are slaves kept in line on a measly wage that is enough to sustain life but little more. It is, in fact, an existence, and even the Maheu mother admits that one of the main reasons to have children is so they can grow, get a job at the mine and bring in a wage. It doesn't help of course that the work is backbreaking, tough and highly dangerous. A change is definitely in order, but it's the method applied to making that change which remains up for debate.

Germinal is not, however, a message movie, and is far from preaching. It resists the urge to bark socialist slogans at the audience, but does yearn for a world where things are shared more evenly and where the rich don't conserve quite so much. (There is a telling scene when, after taking a basket of food to Mabheu's family home, the rich gentleman makes sure the young girl doesn't leave the basket behind.) The saddest part of it all is the fact that the predicaments faced by the people of this story, over a century into the past, are just as familiar today. We need only watch the news to prove that.

Germinal was a hugely important film in its day, the most expensive French production up to that time (Berri and Depardieu's earlier collaboration, Jean de Florette, had previously been France's highest budgeted film in 1986), and a massive box office hit, bringing in over 6 million viewers in French cinemas. It received numerous Cesar nominations, including Best Film and Best Actor for Gerard, but only won for its admittedly brilliant cinematography by Yves Angelo and the costumes.

Roger Ebert gave the film 3 out of 4, noting, "The film will seem filled with unrelieved gloom for many audience members. There are also some unplanned smiles - as when the hefty Depardieu is sponging down, and we cannot help observing that he, at least, doesn't seem to be underfed. The overall effect of the movie is much the same as the effect of Zola's novel: To present a time and place so realistically in fiction that the audience will be able to share the experience. For me, "Germinal" provided visual and dramatic images for 19th century history events that I only understood in an abstract way."

The LA Times were more impressed and less superficial in their response: "Claude Berri's soaring, magnificent film of Emile Zola's Germinal cuts right to the movies' unique, paradoxical power of rendering human misery at its most unrelenting with images of surpassing grandeur and meaning. Pictures don't get much bleaker than this 158-minute epic saga of the grinding existence of 19th-Century French coal miners - but they don't get much more beautiful either. Since Germinal is so determinedly grim and the socioeconomic ills and injustices it depicts so depressingly familiar, one might well ask why one should submit to it - and submission, make no mistake about it, is precisely what is required. The answer is that we can see ourselves in the film's people and be moved by their plight, buoyed by their warm, earthy spirit and thrilled by how vividly Berri has brought the past back to life. Germinal offers only the most tentative note of hope, but that it was made in the first place is in itself an act of affirmation."

The New York Times wrote, "Germinal may be hobbled by obviousness, but it remains a formidable accomplishment. Mr. Berri does succeed in capturing the novel's sweep, and he never minimizes its sense of purpose. Even when set forth in the multi-million-dollar language of present-day film making, the hard facts of this story have enduring force. Mr. Berri keeps the story's violence abrupt and shocking just as Zola did, which has the effect of magnifying its pent-up rage." They added that Gerard gave "another astonishingly honest and unaffected performance..."

Germinal is one of the finest films Depardieu has appeared in, a masterpiece of visuals, performance, moralising and storytelling, that will make you cry, laugh, gasp and rear back in horror from the darkness of human behaviour at its most raw.

THE MAN IN THE IRON MASK (1998)

Though certainly not Depardieu's finest film, his part in The Man in the Iron Mask is an important stop in the great man's rich and varied filmography. Firstly, it's a big film in the truest sense, a Hollywood epic blockbuster which was quite a big deal at the time, especially as it starred the hottest new star of the era, Leonardo DiCaprio. Secondly, it's a well made, competent action adventure movie in its own right. And thirdly, Depardieu has a great part in it, and is, predictably enough, absolutely brilliant. He plays the part of Porthos, one of the iconic musketeers, now ageing but still glorious in the era of Louis XIV. The other musketeers are played by John Malkovich, Jeremy Irons and Gabriel Byrne (the latter as D'Artagnan), while DiCaprio tackles the dual role of the spoilt Luois XIV and his brother.

Directed, written and produced by Randall Wallace, this 35 million dollar epic was a huge hit at the time, released as it was in the wake of Titanic, the motion picture extravaganza that made a mega star of DiCaprio. He is a competent leading man, but at this stage he lacked the depth of his more recent work, most of which is down to age and experience. The best work here though comes from the ageing musketeers, out of retirement for their latest mission. Byrne is brilliant as D'Artagnon, but in my view Depardieu walks away with the picture, charisma personified in a role which looks cartoonish on paper but is given extra dimension by Gerard.

In my view, the film looks overdone now and is very much stuck in its era, the late 1990s. This was the period in which Hollywood came up with the idea that the more money you throw into a picture the better it will be. Fortunately, The Man in the Iron Mask has enough wit and charm to lift it above its often pointless extravagance and silliness.

Many reviewers found the film slow to start with and its over reliance on so called crudity, most of it centring around Depardieu's boorish character, tiresome. Variety noted, "it gets off to a worrisome start with a barrage of crude anatomical humour, involving the gamy roisterer Porthos, aimed directly at a 90s teen sensibility. Tone remains uncertain for the first reel or two... But once DiCaprio almost single handedly hoists the film above ground, these concerns fall by the wayside as the high level intrigue and melodrama take hold." Funnily enough, such reviews, perhaps typical of American critics, are the complete opposite of how I myself viewed the picture. I found the more meandering opening, complete with that silly old thing called character development, much more interesting than the plot that ensues, but each to their own.

The Man in the Iron Mask is good old fashioned, solid entertainment, not something to be taken remotely serious, but a movie that deserves to be looked back upon, if not just for nostalgia, but to enjoy the interactions of the grizzled musketeers.

THE COUNT OF MONTE CRISTO (1998)

Though a blasphemous statement (yet a true one), Gerard Depardieu was once a God in France, a man who could do no wrong, who embodied their homeland and was the son they were most proud of. Today he is still an icon, but one who divides the locals. Across the world he is mostly known for things which undermine his genius work on the screen; for being a wild man, a pisser on aeroplanes, a friend of Putin, a devourer of food and wine. What work he is known for is sparse, films like Green Card and Cyrano de Bergerac, or the lesser films like the Asterix series (likeable films in my view), the Hollywood blockbusters like 1492 and The Man in the Iron Mask, or the downright awful 102 Dalmatians. Thankfully, one of his most loved pieces of work is no doubt the 1998 miniseries The Count Of Monte Cristo, which proved to be a TV hit all over the world.

Depardieu plays Edmond Dantes, a man accused, falsely, of Bonapartism. He is locked up in the Chateau d'If, an island prison like Alcatraz from which no man has ever escaped. When he meets fellow prisoner Abbe Faria (Georges Moustaki), the supposed madman reveals his plans to retrieve a loot of buried treasure on another island. When Abbe dies, Edmond disguises himself as the corpse to escape from the prison and makes his way to the island to dig out the treasure. Once free he plans to use his wealth to get his own back on those who did him wrong.

Fans of Depardieu will find The Count of Monte Cristo a delight. Not only does it give them a chance to see Gerard in a truly brilliant role, but also the opportunity to observe him in six hours of high quality television. This is no cheap TV corn-fest, this is as good as if not better than anything they could have shot on to the big screen. Didier Decoin adapted Alexandre Dumas's novel with style, while director Josee Dayan ensures proceedings remain both epic and personal. Depardieu gives a performance I feel could be placed amongst his twenty best, while the beautiful Ornella Muti, Gerard's co star over twenty years earlier in Marco Ferreri's outrageous The Last Woman, is excellent as Mercedes. Still, this is Gerard's show completely.

The series did well everywhere, and even when reviewers found parts of the story lacking, they never faulted the power of Depardieu. The Los Angeles Times wrote in their review, "Congratulations, too, on that fine actor Depardieu, a perfect choice for the wounded but obsessed Edmond. Depardieu has a great affinity for unpretentious, flesh and blood figures, and as Edmond he projects hurt one moment, menace the next. Your characters may be one-dimensional, Alexandre, but Depardieu isn't."

Some say this is the last truly great performance Depardieu gave, which is of course utter drivel. He has been consistently brilliant in the twenty two years since, particularly in The Singer, Welcome to New York, Mammuth, The Valley of Love and Marseilles. But this is a formidable performance all the same, a tour de force of screen acting that no other performer could have pulled off. Again, it's in the mixture of moods and emotions, the way he can bounce from anger to vulnerability from one moment to another. Absolutely essential.

BETWEEN STRANGERS (2002)

Though Gerard Depardieu's role in Between Strangers is very brief indeed, the film as a whole is one of the most effective ones he has appeared in during the past twenty years. Directed and written by Edoardo Ponti (son of Sophia Loren), this wonderful ensemble drama is set in Toronto and contains various tales going on in fairly close proximity, culminating in a moment when the three main characters accidentally encounter each other amidst their life changing experiences.

Among the tales is one featuring the great Sophia Loren herself as a tragically put upon and hopelessly frustrated wife of the cold Pete Postlethwaite. In public she cares for her harsh, wheel chair bound husband, being on the brunt of his abuse more often than not. In private however she can be seen drawing the most beautiful pictures, a therapeutic act that soothes the loss of her daughter who she gave up for adoption years earlier. But her arty ambitions are brushed off by her distant, heartless husband. Depardieu plays a kindly gardener of a park where she sits and sketches, who listens to her worries and generally cheers her up. He is not a vital part of her plot, but provides important relief in her life. Effortlessly it seems, Depardieu makes the man come alive. Had the film been made in Hollywood however, Depardieu's part would have likely been fleshed out into love interest for the ageing housewife. Thankfully this is no traditional American film and as it is, Loren and Depardieu's tale, also aided by a fine turn from Postlethwaite, is a subtle thing of wonder.

In another tale, Deborah Kara Unger is a divorced woman who meets her father (Malcolm McDowell in one of his most restrained, humourless, sad roles) after he is released from a 20 year prison sentence for killing Unger's mum. She struggles tragically with the tug of war of emotions within herself, moments away from shooting her monstrous dad, but also toying with killing herself too. For me this was the most powerful yet upsetting of the films' tales. The third story concerns Mira Sorvino as a young photographer following in her harsh, aspirational father's footsteps. She lands her first Time cover story, a close up portrait of a young girl in a war torn country. Though proud of her work, she is also conflicted with guilt and is desperate to know the fate of the poor child whose face has earned her a sizeable career boost.

The film has a rather unshowy, unspectacular feel, which works in its favour, and is directed with simplicity by Edoardo. The performances here make this one of the best ensemble casts ever; Unger, an underrated talent, is absolutely fantastic, and we feel her anguish throughout; McDowell surprises us with a totally uncharacteristic part, wallowing in self hatred and guilt while attempting to rebuild a bridge with his daughter who despises him for what he did; Depardieu, though deserving of more screen time, gives the film a bit of joy, which it certainly needs. The best performance however comes from Loren, both proud and put upon, a woman underappreciated by others but who will find the inner strength to rise above her controlling husband and blossom into who she should be. It's a towering effort, right up there with her best performances.

It received a 10 minute standing ovation after its premiere at the Venice Film Festival, though it mostly attracted unfairly negative reviews in the press. Variety found it no better than an average TV movie and found the performances stilted, save for one: "Script cycles smoothly from one cliche to another, relying on the cast's famous faces to create interest in the undeveloped characters. The only perf with a core of realism comes from Postlethwaite, who suggests that John's monstrous egotism and repressive personality may have subtle roots in his wife's attitude. Loren, fascinating as ever to observe on screen, wears a mask of Greek tragedy even when stocking shelves in a supermarket; Unger is similarly directed to go Hellenic in her homicidal hatred for Dad. As the young photographer with moral qualms, Sorvino is a tad more restrained, while Depardieu, Brandauer and McDowell basically act on cue."

Between Strangers is a great chance to watch an all star cast not dazzle, sparkle or stun, but quietly impress with the kind of roles they might not have ever played had Edoardo and Sophia not convinced them all to get involved. Hugely under-appreciated, and now lost in time, this buried gem is well worth tracking down for both fans of the leading players and anyone interested in carefully measured drama, acted with grace and class.

Cannes Film Festival, 1991

NATHALIE (2003)

Anne Fontaine's subtly erotic drama Nathalie is a prime example of how understatement, ambiguity and restraint can make for a more gripping film than one that chooses to go for the obvious and expected. It is worth considering that when they remade this film in America, they turned a tale of quiet, masochistic obsession into an all out erotic thriller, with everything turned up to eleven and the added disadvantage of zero subtlety. That remake, titled Chloe and starring Julianne Moore, was OK in its own way, but is certainly a more typically American take on the theme of jealousy creating the problem.

The original, and much better film, stars Fanny Ardant as Catherine, a middle aged gynaecologist who finds out that her husband Bernard (Depardieu) has been enjoying the flesh of other women. Ever more suspicious of him, she hires a high class prostitute (played by Emmanuelle Beart) to come on to him in his favourite cafe and feed back information on what went on and what was said. Using the name Nathalie, the young professional is paid regularly by Catherine for her time with her husband. While at first she is terribly jealous when hearing their so called sessions together, which quickly turn sexual, she eventually begins to become weirdly interested and quietly infatuated with Nathalie herself. It is clear after a while that these thoughts turn to genuine feelings, but can Nathalie truly be trusted, and is what she says totally true?

Nathalie is a smooth, seamless drama that has a calm eroticism burning through it, but is never explicit, nor does it lower itself to the obvious mechanisms of the genre. It is a film made successful by carefully played performances, none of which ever veer from tastefulness. Ardant carries the film as the quiet wife, so conservative on the centre but secretly aroused by the seamier world she soon finds herself in. Depardieu is at his least aggressive here, playing a busy husband who, though not against the odd fling, is a good husband 90 percent of the time. Perhaps the finest performance here though comes from Beart, sexy in an unassuming way, retaining her mystery and enigma as the appealing lady of the night finding herself in the most unusual situation from which she is sure to benefit.

Nathalie attracted some praise but mostly critical negativity. Peter Bradshaw of the Guardian found it overdone, pretentious and bordering on spoof: "The sheer smugness of this movie, its fatuous belief in how daringly sophisticated it is, can't be overestimated. It is like a nightmare parody of French cinema with almost every visual and dramatic cliche present and correct: the frostily reserved moments in the marital home, the snatched glances in the cafe, the hotel bed linen's post-coital disorder. This is one to forget."

Slant Magazine seemed to hate it, writing, "Its conceit one of pure fantasy, Fontaine's film exists in some sort of bizarre alternate reality in which Depardieu might have a shot at successfully seducing Béart, Ardant would actually pay a woman to screw her husband as a means of learning what turns him (and herself!) on, and women of the night are actually beautiful college graduates who only ply their wares in the flesh industry during off-hours from their respectable beauty salon jobs. Whatever it is that Fontaine and co-screenwriters Jacques Fieschi and François-Olivier Rousseau think they're saying about fidelity and desire gets hopelessly obscured by the absurdity of their scenario and condescension toward their audience."

While the ending does lean towards a troubling kind of consequence-free conservatism, if not downright denial, Nathalie is an intriguing study of mistrust, desire and masochism.

SINGER (2006)

One of the less expected gems of Depardieu's 21st century output is The Singer, also known as When I Was A Singer, a warm and often moving drama with Gerard at his charismatic best. Written and directed by Xavier Giannoli, it stars Depardieu as Alain Moreau, an old fashioned crooner who with his competent but rather dated backing band plays dance halls for an ageing female audience. To people under a certain age, he is unknown, but to his adoring, largely female fanbase he is a legend, a loveable ladies' man. He is popular in this crowd and posters of his gigs, featuring Alain in a corny white suit holding a rose, are plastered all over town. The problem is, Alain can see his style of music is fading into the past, and as fewer people seem to be turning up to his shows, he is aware he is in danger of becoming completely obsolete. Yet he makes a decent living, with his ex girlfriend acting as his loyal manager.

One night at a show he meets Marion (Cecil De France), a colleague of his estate agent friend Bruno (Mathieu Amalric) who Alain is smitten with. They end up spending the night together, but she leaves in the morning without saying goodbye. Feeling humiliated, Alain visits her at work under the pretence that he is looking for a new property. A friendship develops, and though Marion, who has a troubled life and a son to her ex partner, at first relents the older man's gentle advances, she begins to soften and develop genuine feelings for him.

The Singer is a sensitive, careful film, but it is not in the least schmaltzy. As Alain is a corny singer, the film is full of cheesy music, but none of it is used for corny effect, more poignantly. This ageing dance hall crooner may be heading over the hill, but he's not ready to slide down it just yet. Ever aware of the possibility that work may dry up, Marion gives him a new lease of life, and in the end he accepts what he is, that he is comfortable as a dance hall singer (he does get a support slot at an arena gig but decides to leave slyly before the show begins) and the big break which has alluded him all his life is not his destiny. But will he and Marion end up together? This is left until the film's final moments.

Giannoli's script is subtle and understated, never forcing overcooked melodrama down ones throat. There is also a distinct lack of predictability, with all cliches avoided. Marion is no perfect young woman, and though we like Alain, Giannoli decides we are not to pity the man. Alain knows who he is, is very aware of himself and his situation, and is certainly no man to feel sorry for. His work is well paid, he has a certain cult following, and the film makes no attempt to turn him into a figure of fun.

The direction is unfussy, giving the actors room to breathe and flesh out their roles. Cecile De France is effective as Marion, a conflicted and contradictory woman, and the supporting players are good too, especially Christine Citti as Alain's manager, his rock in many ways. Obviously though, the finest work is from Depardieu, delivering a rich and believable performance. He becomes the lounge singer, embodying the cheesiness of such a veteran but being careful not to make him a tragic figure. Depardieu makes Alain likeable, and avoids cynicism. Though there are niggles of dissatisfaction from time to time, he is a perfectly realistic man. His pining for Marion is wonderfully played too, never forcing himself on the woman who is so clearly attracted to him but reluctant to take the big step. Depardieu's performance is one of the finest in recent years. Many critics regarded it his best performance since Cyrano de Bergerac after what some called a period lacking inspiration. It has to be said that he hadn't been outstanding since perhaps The Count of Monte Cristo, though he had been in good films in the period between the miniseries and The Singer. In all honesty though, his Alain is one of the sharpest characterisations he's given us in the past thirty years.

Asked by Girl.com what attracted him to the picture, Depardieu said "it was very beautiful and written by someone who knew what he was talking about. The authenticity of the dialogue reminded me of the films that I love. It is stamped with a very poetic respect for dance hall singers in Clermont-Ferrand or anywhere else. I didn't see in it the condescending, metropolitan attitude that a lot of pretentious young directors would have shown. Then I saw Xavier leading a crew that he seemed to be used to working with, demanding the highest standards of everybody without being overbearing."

On his character, Depardieu explained, "Alain Moreau is a man who likes tunes and songs and who simply makes people dance. In this instance, it wasn't any tougher to perform Gainsbourg's songs than Christophe's or anybody else's. The whole point wasn't to mimic them but to play Alain Moreau performing them in his own way."

Depardieu seems to have understood Alain completely, a man he clearly likes which is evident in his sympathetic portrayal. "He knows that world, but he prefers his small world of people who come to dance to him. He knows that he can never be a star. Does he actually want to be one? Isn't that what makes him so different, so human? He lives with his goat, his sun lamp, and his melancholy. The only thing that can upset his solitude is love."

Gerard was not pretentious about his role and though aware the film was sentimental in tone, he saw no problem in that. Speaking to the European film press, Gerard explained his view: "I don't understand the idea of wanting to avoid sentiment, theatricality, the clown. I love melodramas. And Xavier Giannoli did not shy away from sentiment, nor did he wallow in it. There's an honesty in showing feelings that are noble and I for one live out my feelings. It's rare to find topics where all you have to do is "be", because we cannot act everything, contrary to what many people think. I've noticed that films that express a reality, the truth, are always more popular, even if, and it is unfortunate to have to say this, there are few scripts like that."

The Singer received wide acclaim upon release, lauded at Cannes and nominated for their Golden Palm Award. Depardieu also received a Cesar nomination, as did the film itself. After appearing in some films which a few critics thought were undeserving of him, if not being totally undignified for an actor as powerful as he, The Singer was seen as a comeback, a return to the glory of old for the great Depardieu. Anyone who works as much as Depardieu does (in 2002 alone he appeared in 8 films, then in seven the following year), there are bound to be some duds. In 2006 he appeared in the awful American film The Last Holiday, and also popped up for a brief cameo in Paris, je t'aime. The Singer then, the only other movie he appeared in that year, seems to have taken up a lot of his creative energy. And it shows, for this is a tour de force of control and he never loses focus for a single second. A lesser actor might have turned him into a caricature (even the modern De Niro would have been incapable of making Alain such a realistic character), but Gerard gives him multi dimensions, both melancholic and reasonably happy with his situation; again, a man plodding on but unexpectedly falling in a kind of love which threatens his complacency.

Peter Bradshaw, ever a fan of Depardieu, wrote in the Guardian that Gerard miraculously hadn't changed all that much since his seventies heyday, and called it "a return to form, and a lovely, if self-conscious, performance... Depardieu is great as Alain. A gentle, autumnal film, with nice performances from Depardieu and De France."

Paul Griffiths of Eye For Film gave it 4 stars, writing, "Gerard Depardieu is so good as The Singer that I can almost forgive his besmirching those childhood memories with the travesties of the Asterix and Obellix movies. His turn as a low-key dance hall and wedding reception crooner is an understated, believably layered and textured performance. It's a healthy reminder of the unequivocal natural force that Depardieu can summon when he's in focus and on target. It isn't for nothing that praise such as 'a real return to form' has been bandied around since the film was nominated for the Golden Palm at last year's Cannes festival."

The Singer is just a genuinely good film, not one needing to resort to swearing, violence, sex or shock tactics (though those elements can enrich a film too), but relying on charm and two truly extraordinary characterisations. A film not to be overlooked.

LA VIE EN ROSE (2007)

Not only is La Vie en rose one of the most acclaimed and successful French films of all time, it is also one of the finest biopics ever made. Retelling the life of iconic French singer Edith Piaf, it stars Marion Cotillard as the legend herself, delivering a spellbinding performance which rightly won her the Oscar. It is indeed a towering effort, with Cotillard embodying Piaf to a tee, but La Vie en rose succeeds on every other level too.

Though the film begins in 1959, one night while Piaf is singing in concert, it goes into flashback almost immediately. We are at the tail end of the First World War, and Edith's mother sings on street corners for pennies. She wants to be a star, so writes to Edith's father, a circus performer still in the trenches, to say that she is giving the girl up so she can pursue her career. But the father doesn't want her either, at least for the moment, and he leaves her with his own mother, a madam who runs a brothel. She warms to one prostitute in particular, Titine, a volatile redhead who adores Edith. Though she enjoys her time there and strikes up a bond with the girls, it is hardly the ideal environment for a child. Suddenly, her dad turns up and takes Edith away.

In between flashbacks, we see the late fifties Edith, dining with friends, where dark secrets are revealed, though the narrative never stays on these sequences for too long, zooming back in time again to reveal the hard times the famous singer has behind her. We see the infamous vision she had of St Therese, before her first performance; it's an impromptu song she entertains folk with while her father's street act flops. Piaf realises the power she has when singing, and how it makes her feel in control of the moment. We then see Piaf growing up, singing on the streets just like her mother, with her friend Momone. She is hired by club owner Louis Leplee, played by Gerard Depardieu, the first man to see her potential and nickname her "Piaf" because she is like a little sparrow. Though experiencing some negative feedback at first, she begins to build a name and reputation for herself on the stage. The film continues to flit between her rise to stardom and her later years, bed ridden and suffering from the effects of alcoholism, though the film itself ends on a high note, despite the tragic end of the star.

Director Olivier Dahan guides the viewer through this remarkable life, floating in and out of time spans effortlessly, ensuring the viewer gets to soak up the atmosphere of each era and the beauty and tragedy of key events in Piaf's life. The screenplay by Dahan and Isabelle Sobelman avoids cliches, but does not shy away from the true horror of Edith's struggles. It is harsh without being unfeeling, tragic without pulling at the heart strings, presenting Piaf's life as it was. At the centre of this cleverly structured and wonderfully presented film is a truly astonishing performance from Cotillard, who was cast by the director before he even met her, because he saw something in her eyes that immediately made him think of Edith. The producer Alain Goldman fought Cotillard's corner despite protests from the distributors, but luckily they were eventually won over. It is impossible to imagine anyone else in the role, and the tour de force is surely one of the greatest performances of the last thirty or more years.

Though Depardieu's role is relatively small in the scope of the film, it is a hugely important one. He is the man who discovers her, brings her off the streets and into the bohemian, artistic, fun loving society, gives her a chance at success and believes in her. He is her "Daddy Leplee", her saviour in many ways, who arrives hatted and in a long coat to save her from poverty - the sad fate of her mother which she wanted to avoid - and help give her a proper life. When he is murdered, Piaf is devastated, but is also blamed for his death. They call her a bad omen, a curse, and she is even arrested due to her mob connections. Depardieu, in his brief section of the picture, is quietly effective as the warm and open club owner, making his death another tragic event in a life full of them; her mother's rejection, being snatched from the brothel, the father's failings, Leplee's death... Anyone who cares for or hopes to protect Piaf is snatched away cruelly. Even her friend Momone, at one point the only true friend she has, is taken from her. But Depardieu had to be in the film for other reasons; not just because he's French and has a habit of being in the biggest films France produces, but because he's their most famous export, and surely he deserved to be a part of a biopic of a true French icon.

Cotillard not only won the Oscar for Best Actress (the second French actress to do so) she also won a Golden Globe, BAFTA, Cesar, the Czech Lion and the Prix Lumiere gong, basically every plaudit any serious actress would wish to take home with her. The film itself was nominated at the Cesars, the BAFTAs and all over the world, while also becoming a box office hit in every country it was released. La Vie en rose tells a compelling (and true) story, is enthralling all the way through, but the one element which sticks out from the rest is undoubtedly Cotillard's perfect performance. The strength of the picture relied on whoever played Piaf, naturally, and a lesser talent, perhaps a better known actress, could surely not have embodied the icon as Marion did. It truly is worth the price of admission alone.

Though there were some snotty reviews in the UK (the Guardian's Peter Bradshaw gave it 2 stars and called it a selective biopic), most reviews were positive. Roger Ebert called it on of the best biopics he had ever seen, and I have to agree. It may not be a conventional life story, but it is a very engaging and imaginative one. It does not attempt to answer questions about Piaf's turbulent life, one which consistently experienced highs and lows together, elation going hand in hand with heartbreaking tragedy throughout the years. But by avoiding cliches and the "normal" way a biopic is explored (especially in Hollywood), by not theorising and coming to ludicrous conclusions, it remains free form, open to interpretation and in many ways immortalises Piaf more than a standard biopic might have. By flitting between childhood, mid-period and the final years, it makes Piaf's life equally important at each stage, the icon who was born a star even before she was known all over the world. A masterclass in telling a life story, La Vie en rose is something to behold.

MAMMUTH (2010)

For all the talk that Depardieu hasn't appeared in a decent film in years, being a shadow of his former self, or worse a parody, these critics surely haven't been playing close attention to the man's career - for want of a better word. Mammuth is evidence that Gerard still takes risks and agrees to play roles that are challenging, thought provoking and daring. It would be easy for a man like Depardieu to take the big bucks, appear in anything offering him enough money and get complacent. On the contrary, Depardieu takes roles which interest him, no matter the size of the budget or pay check.

Mammuth was written and directed by Benoit Delepine and Gustave de Kervern. It stars Depardieu as Serge, a sixty year old slaughterhouse worker who, when hitting sixty, retires after many years of service. His retirement party, perhaps the crappest send off known to man, involves his colleagues munching crisps, wearing blood stained garments, as the manager performs an underwhelming speech, at the end of which Serge is given a jigsaw. Returning home, Serge is stuck for what to do with his new found spare time. When he messes up the shopping and locks himself in the bathroom after trying to fix the door, his wife (played by Yolande Moreau) tells him to visit the pension office to see about getting his monthly payments. It is then he discovers that he doesn't have enough pay slips to claim his pension. Heading out on his old beloved motorbike, which he names Mammuth, Serge embarks on a surreal road trip to fill in his employment gaps. Along the way he experiences many memorable things, reliving his memories and making new ones.

Mammuth is one of those films which contains so many hilarious and unforgettable scenes that every moment is a highlight. It's a film which develops and grows as Serge learns more about himself. A key developments comes when Serge visits his brother's house, to learn he is not there, but his niece is. Miss Ming plays Solange, his brother's eccentric daughter, who develops a meaningful bond with Serge and helps him grasp the truth of his own life and place on this earth. One of the more unexpected scenes comes when Serge is excited by the news that his cousin is living up stairs, above where Solange does her bizarre art. The two long lost relatives embrace, two older men enjoying their reunion; we have seen this kind of moving moment many times, though it is altered drastically when we quickly cut away to the cousins in bed providing each other hand relief. Mammuth is full with such scenes, though it never seems over stuffed, nor does the strange eccentricity seem forced. It's an organic, hugely enjoyable though admittedly often outrageous ride across modern France, a country seen through the eyes of a man whose better days are behind him, but also has a lot to look forward to.

Depardieu is magnificent as Serge, a long haired retiree bumbling along, failing to see where he fits into the world now he is without employment He is a man of yesteryear, out of place in a land that is now cynical and more complicated than the one he once knew. He is also haunted by the ghost of his ex girlfriend (played by Depardieu's old co star, the wonderful Isabelle Adjani), who died on the back of his motorcycle decades earlier. Her face, with those famous wide open eyes and blood streaking across it, is eerily haunting and she provides the film with a poetic edge that blunts the jagged, often broad humour. It is a perfectly balanced film, featuring fine performances, poignant sequences and a pace which never becomes tiring.

Gerard told journalists upon the film's release that he related closely to the part. Abandoning that famous fire present in so many of his iconic roles, he gives a Serge a subtle, restrained gentleness, making him one of his most appealing and warm characters. Depardieu said he was inspired by his own father's humble life and brought personal touches to Serge. It is also worth noting that Depardieu apparently didn't even receive pay for the film, according to Kervern.

The filmmakers took part in an illuminating interview for Cineuropa's website, and on collaborating with Depardieu, Benoit Delepine said, "Working with Gérard is really great. He knows all about technique since he's worked on 400 films throughout his career. You don't have to tell him much. He knows what has to be done and in the end he directed his own character. We didn't have much choice when it came to Gérard's look. He didn't want to change his hairstyle, even though he's done this often during his career. We needed an ageing biker look, which was incompatible with his usual haircut. The wig and other additions were found at the last minute. It was very difficult imposing all that on Gérard, but it was important for him to change because his character also changes in the film."

It was clear the duo had an enormous amount of respect for the iconic Gerard. Kervern noted, "He often joked about his body when he saw himself like that on screen, but we thought he was magnificent. He's a big fat lion, but a total lion nonetheless."

Though nominated for the Silver Bear Award, it received a somewhat mixed reaction from critics. In the UK however, Peter Bradshaw loved it, writing in the Guardian, "Kervern and Delépine have an unmatched ability to spring something new on the viewer, to keep you off balance, and there is one jaw-dropping scene which shows Depardieu engaging in the kind of recreational activity which certainly never featured in Green Card... there is a consistent level of comic invention, with plenty of laugh-out-loud moments" Of Gerard, he concluded with "Depardieu is an enigma, too. He can be conceited and frankly terrible in some films – I shudder to think about him in Last Holiday, with Queen Latifah – but sometimes that great barrage-balloon figure, paunchy in both body and face, fills the screen gloriously. This is his best role since the has-been lounge singer in Xavier Giannoli's Quand J'etais Chanteur. There could be a rich new seam in bittersweet comedies for Depardieu to mine."

In the US it seemed to trouble certain critics, who found it grubby and crusty looking. Variety thought Mammuth a quirky mixed bag, dubbing it "an unsatisfying if occasionally amusing hybrid attempt by the helmer-scribes to maintain their offbeat humor while providing an emotional underpinning. Shot on reversible Super 16 for a grainy 1970s look, the pic relies heavily on Gerard Depardieu's consummate but sagging shoulders while basically wasting national treasure Yolande Moreau. Energy is maintained in the first half as just-retired Depardieu hits the road to find former employers, but the rest wilts under a mishmash of confused sentiment. With long, stringy hair and a large physical ease, Depardieu certainly inhabits his role, getting under the skin of this doltish but sincere figure looking for something to fill his life."

Mammuth is, for me, a success on every level. This is a new Depardieu, a battered but not beaten man with hints of sadness and regret. Beneath his tough exterior though is a fundamentally decent man, someone who has coasted through life on a kind of auto pilot and only now when faced with retirement and the prospects of crumbling away does he realise who he is. The film mixes hand held rawness with a hazy, nostalgic lens for flashbacks and scenes evocative of Serge's youth, making it completely unique visually as well as content-wise. In a book that hopes to span all the finest work from Depardieu's long and rich 50 year plus career, there is no way a film this enjoyable, funny, deep and subtly bittersweet could be skimmed over. A truly wonderful experience.

LIFE OF PI (2012)

Life of Pi is without doubt one of the most acclaimed and popular serious films of the past decade, and also the biggest film, budget and success wise, Gerard Depardieu has ever appeared in. He may not be a major character or a driving force throughout, but his presence is important. The film itself, one might say, belongs entirely to Ang Lee, who working from David Magee's smart screenplay (itself based on the book by Yann Martel) has created a modern masterpiece, utilising the best in CGI to enhance, not lead, his story. It is beautifully acted and is an epic in the truest sense of the word.

The film starts when a writer is sent to speak to Piscine Molitor, after a friend informs him that the man's life would make an interesting book. Seated before him at a table, "Pi" begins to tell the tale of his varied life. To recount every event here would ruin the film for anyone who hasn't seen it, but in general it starts with his childhood, the zoo his family owned, and the move to Canada when Pi is 16. When heading across the sea, the boat containing the family and all the animals in containers is damaged during a storm and Pi finds himself alone on a lifeboat. After witnessing the primal urges of various animals, such as the zebra, the orangutan and a vicious hyena, he begins to fish in order to survive. Then comes the personification of his primal form, in the embodiment of a tiger, a beast he must wrestle with, psychologically, but ultimately work alongside in order to survive. He spends 227 days on board the lifeboat, with only a Bengal tiger for company, in what becomes a parable of perseverance, single mindedness and survival.

In its original development stage, M Night Shyamalan was lined up to direct, but thankfully in 2009 Fox hired the great Ang Lee instead. Lee saw the film as a meditation on faith, the water containing life and "every emotion for Pi. And air is God, heaven and something spiritual and death." The sea, vast and cruel, but also beautiful and pure, becomes a metaphor for the world, for life itself. The film, as Lee said, is not religious, but about the power of God, of faith and belief. He directs in a manner which makes the visuals truly awe inspiring, but only in what they contain. A film can look as good as you like, with budget permitting, but to add meaning to the visuals is another matter all together. This beautiful and poetic film is dazzling to watch but most of the power is internal, comes from within, as Pi proves throughout his struggle.

Depardieu, another vital face in the international cast Lee was committed to hiring, has a small role as a nasty French chef on board the doomed ship. Of his part, and the film, Depardieu told ST Media, "The chef is not in the book, but he (Lee) did a good adaptation. The situation is an unusual one but a wonderful one." The chef, though a brief character, seems to embody all that is wrong with humanity, though one wishes Depardieu, as brilliant as he is here, could have been on screen a little more. As he is not central to the film's predicament, it seems ill fitting to this book, one about Depardieu's finest performances, to go into too much detail; but ignoring this modern classic would be misguided at best.

Life of Pi was a huge success in every area, making 600 million at the box office, receiving countless awards and nominations, not to mention some of the best reviews of 2012. Roger Ebert called it "a miraculous achievement of storytelling and a landmark of visual mastery. I have decided it is one of the best films of the year." Once again, Ebert had a point.

THE ASTERIX AND OBELIX MOVIES (1999 - 2012)

Though the films themselves cannot be compared to Depardieu's finest work, and they do often get a hard time from critics, the Asterix and Obelix films cannot be ignored when looking at the scope of Gerard's long and winding on screen career. They have, after all, been immensely popular all over the world, and made it so Depardieu can be recognised by millions of children on any street across the globe. They are also, I might add, good fun, a relief if you like, amidst the more intense and challenging films he has been a part of.

Based on the comics by Albert Uderzo and Rene Gosciny, the series follows Asterix and Obelix, plus the occupants of their French village, who have managed to keep out the Roman army thanks to a potion created by their druid, Getafix, which keeps them strong and able to fight their oppressors. When it eventually came to the idea of converting these cartoon strips to celluloid, there really was no better actor to play Obelix, the oversized side kick to Asterix, than Gerard Depardieu. Looking again at the original drawings and it seems, impossible as it is, that the character was based on Depardieu.

The first picture was released in 1999, entitled Asterix and Obelix Take On Caesar. Pulling together various plots from the series of comics, it was directed by Claude Zidi, produced by the great Claude Berri and was, at the time, the most expensive French production in the history of their cinema (Depardieu had a habit of appearing in the biggest French films, even if he often leant towards arthouse productions). The film is great for kids, has some genuine laughs, is nicely directed and features some outstanding set pieces. The main reason to watch it though, for adults at least, is for the casting; Christian Clavier is splendid as Asterix, while Depardieu embodies Obelix the way he had Rodin, Jean de Florette, Martin Guerre and his vast gallery of iconic faces. Obelix is a remarkable character in himself; as a child he fell into a pot of potion which means he has a superhuman strength. But he is a warm man, funny, a little dopey, and extremely likeable. The idea of Gerard dressed as Obelix might have seemed absurd before the films themselves were made, but as soon as one sees Depardieu, with that trademark nose of his, with ginger wig and familiar costume, it works extremely well. With his large appetite, lust for life and bold manner, Depardieu and Obelix are like long lost brothers.

The picture was well received, and had the added bonus of the great Roberto Benigni's presence, a man who never fails to entertain. Though hugely budgeted at 42 million dollars, it made over 100 million back at the box office. Empire Magazine wrote of the film, "In creating a new, more multi-layered storyline, writer/director Zidi manages to address any concerns over durability and the cast do well in rounding out their creations: Depardieu is in hearty form, Benigni brings his trademark to le party, whilst the standout is Clavier, who cuts an endearing figure behind his huge 'tache."

The second film, perhaps the best, is Asterix and Obelix: Mission Cleopatra, featuring the striking Monica Bellucci as the empress herself. Once again, the pace is speedy, the script full of little gems and there are plenty of opportunities for Depardieu to delight as Obelix, beating up Romans and causing havoc at every opportunity. The film is so likeable that, whether watching alone or with your kids, you'd have to be a grumpy old sod not to enjoy the madness of it all. Besides, Depardieu seems to be enjoying himself. The BBC said Depardieu played the role with gusto, adding "Fans of the original will enjoy seeing René Goscinny and Albert Uderzo's characters brought to life, while younger audiences will no doubt appreciate the tongue-in-cheek nods to Star Wars, The Matrix, and Crouching Tiger, Hidden Dragon."

In 2008 a third film saw release, entitled Asterix at the Olympic Games, only Christian Clavier was replaced by Clovis Cornillac, a decent actor in his own right, but not one to compare with Clavier's portrayal.

Depardieu is as watchable as ever, but the film itself seemed weaker, less committed than the first two.

The fourth instalment, once again featuring Depardieu but with Edouard Baer as the diminutive hero, was Asterix and Obelix: God Save Britannia, released in 2012. It was definitely the weakest instalment and one has to ask whether it should have been made at all. A fifth film is pencilled in for production, originally intended for September 2020 but more than likely delayed due to the coronavirus. It needs to be added that Depardieu is not involved, and Obelix will be played by Gilles Lellouche.

Those who argue that Depardieu is now a caricature of himself and incapable of the kind of power he exuded in countless roles from the 70s to the early 90s may overlook these films entirely. But for me, they show that Depardieu is a gifted comedian, doesn't take himself too seriously (though his work is serious to him) and excels in mainstream fare as well as more challenging, avant garde material. Granted, they are not the best films ever made, but they are faithful adaptations of the classic comics, and if you grew up reading them as a child, these movies will, if nothing else, be sweetly nostalgic.

Cannes Film Festival, 2015

WELCOME TO NEW YORK (2014)

Abel Ferrara has directed some of the toughest, most confrontational and fearless films of the past thirty plus years. Always getting to the nitty gritty of whatever matter he takes on, whether it be corrupt police in Bad Lieutenant (1992), the trials of the filmmaker in Dangerous Game (1993, or the world of organised crime in The Funeral (1996), Ferrara is incapable of shying away from the truth. In Welcome to New York, he uncovers the sexual corruption and darkness of the political world, in a film so graphic, aggressive and fearless that the Cannes Film Festival denied it an official screening. Of course, it's staggeringly brilliant.

Depardieu plays Devereaux, a powerful political figure, who may or may not be a candidate for French Presidency. From the word go it is clear this man does whatever he pleases, touches whoever he likes and partakes in whatever activity he wishes. Shamefully corrupt, he puts pleasure before business. Meeting up with friends one night in a hotel, he hires some prostitutes and indulges in an evening of sexual debauchery and drug taking. Come the morning, the tired out politician wakes up and gets a shower. When the maid comes in, Devereaux, so used to being able to take whatever he wants, forces himself brutally upon her. Thankfully she flees his terrifying advances and alerts the authorities. Just about to leave New York for his French home, he is arrested on the plane and taken in for questioning. At mercy before the American law system, it is up to his influential and very wealthy wife Simone (Jacqueline Bisset) to get him out of his latest mess.

Welcome to New York is raw filmmaking at its best, a no frills statement about the corruptive nature of power. Filmed in mostly hand held, it is once again photographed by Ferrara's trusty cinematographer, Ken Kelsch, who seems to effortlessly bring Abel's visions to the screen in all their collaborations. The first part of the film, highlighting Depardieu's complacency and sense of privilege, is unrelenting, merciless in fact, and occasionally jaw droppingly shocking. Gerard is fearless here, grunting like a beast during the sex scenes and manhandling the women as if he owns them, which indeed he feels he does. In the second half, he is robbed of the power and also his dignity, at one point being forced to strip naked in the police station when he is degraded like a common criminal. Another filmmaker might have turned the second half into a redemptive epiphany (indeed, as Ferrara did, in a manner, with his masterpiece Bad Lieutenant), but here Abel relents from doing so, with his crooked politician showing no remorse or regret whatsoever. When he is questioned by a psychiatrist, he admits to having no feelings for the women he inflicts his feverish desire upon. Worse still, while we imagine he might have learned a lesson of some sort and may control himself around women in the future, the finale tells us the opposite. Flirting with a female maid, he looks to the camera, deeply, unsettlingly in fact, as if to tell us he will do it all again.

Rightfully so, in some ways, the film proved controversial, and Dominique Strauss Kahn, upon whom the film was based, threatened to sue them for slander. On top of this it did not receive French distribution and was unofficially screened in a tent during Cannes. It ended up being put out on VOD. Speaking upon its release, an untroubled Ferrara said "These guys didn't like the film. I don't think Thierry [Frémaux, artistic director and delegate general   of the Festival de Cannes   ] or these guys had a problem that way. They just didn't like the movie, you know? None of them did. They really didn't like it. And so, that's it. It's their film festival, they can show what they want. If it was my film festival, I show what I want."

In other interviews he was much angrier. To Dissolve he was fuming at the cuts IFC made upon distribution: "As a filmmaker and a human being I detest the destruction of my film Welcome To New York, now being distributed by IFC and Wild Bunch, and exhibited on Showtime and in IFC theaters. Behind all these entities are individuals—in this case Arianna Bocco, Jonathan Sehring and Vincent Maraval—who feel they can deny my contractual right of final cut, which is simply my freedom of expression. Some people wear hoods and carry automatic weapons, others sit behind their desks, but the attack and attempted suppression of the rights of the individual are the same. I will defend the right of free speech till the end and I ask all who believe as I do to not support the showing of this film, on their networks, in their theaters, or wherever."

The film packs a punch and makes a valid point about power, but the strength is largely down to the formidable presence of Depardieu in a daring, often frighteningly bold portrayal. This is not a flattering role, but Depardieu has no inhibitions. When taking on a part like this there is no holding back and few actors, especially ones as famous and revered as Depardieu, could have pulled it off. Ferrara was highly complimentary of Depardieu's work in the film. "Gérard, Gérard, Gérard. He's a force of nature," he said. "He's a brilliant actor. He's everything that you want for that part, in an actor. That's the shame of it, man: When they made those cuts, they destroyed a work of art. It's a work of art, dude, and you cannot fuck it up for a second of it. What's the word for it? I don't know... destroying it! He's allowing himself, as a human being, to merge himself with the character, the same that the director is allowing himself to merge with the performance. And what you have is special, not just to this film, but to every film. I won't judge that. Gérard is precious; he knows that."

The people who did get to see Welcome to New York at the time of release had mixed reactions, though no one was underwhelmed. The Guardian's Peter Bradshaw, one of the few critics brave enough to admit that Depardieu was still giving solid performances, gave the film four stars and wrote, "Abel Ferrara's crazy, sulphurous, toweringly unpleasant Welcome to New York is like an "issue" movie about sexual assault being beamed to cinema screens live from the seventh circle of hell. There are no blurred lines here, no ambiguities, no water-cooler talking points about gradations of consent. This is a brutal, occasionally inelegant film, but it pulls no punches and shines a stark, pitiless light on its subject. What Depardieu himself makes of his character and his own (excellent) performance is something of a mystery. There is a weird pre-emptive, "interview" scene at the beginning in which he explains to a gallery of fictional reporters that he was attracted to the role precisely because the man is so unpleasant, and unpleasant he certainly is: as unpleasant as Ferrara's King of New York, his Bad Lieutenant, and his vampires in The Addiction. He is another creature of the night, strip-mined of all human feeling."

Simon Abrams called the 125 minute cut of the film one of the best movies of the years, while Cinevue called it a King Lear for the 21st century, "brilliantly played by veteran Depardieu". Yes this is Ferrara's film, but most people will remember it for Depardieu's staggering performance. Whatever you make of the film, it's a fact that Gerard is on top form throughout.

VALLEY OF LOVE (2015)

Valley of Love reunites two of France's most iconic film stars, Gerard Depardieu and Isabelle Huppert, who so memorably set the screen alight in 1980s Loulou, directed by the great Maurice Pialat. Throughout Valley of Love, they carry their legacies and pasts with them, and even though Huppert herself said in one interview that the film held no poignancy for her personally, at least on the level that it had her and Gerard on screen together once again after 35 years, there is a deeply moving and poetic edge which ensures this is a more rewarding and enriching experience than if it had starred two lesser talents, or for that matter, been made by Americans. There is no schmaltz, no emotional manipulation; just a straight forward story acted out by two masters.

The plot is simple but leaves room for interpretation; Depardieu and Huppert play two ageing actors, once married to one another, fittingly enough called Isabelle and Gerard. After their son dies, the two meet up for the first time in what appears to be a long while, following instructions in their late son's will. What makes this strange reunion more interesting though, is the fact that it takes place in the sweltering heat of America's Death Valley, and the instructions from beyond the grave themselves are hardly ordinary. The duo have been told to visit key landmarks at precise times, mapped out in detail in letters from their departed son, who insists that they will get one final vision of him if they follow the guide. As the film goes on, the pair learn more about one another, their pasts, their futures and their late son, culminating in an eerie conclusion which though unsettling, is vague enough to inspire the viewer's theories on what actually happened.

Writer-director Guilaume Nicloux first came up with the idea for the movie after visiting Death Valley himself. Upon his return he began what he described as a kind of automatic writing, obviously stirred up by the inspirational location, adding that the story chose him, not the other way round. While he left the script to one side while working on another film, upon coming back to the material he now knew for sure that Huppert and Depardieu would be his stars. During discussions he and Gerard agreed that the character should be as close to the real Depardieu as possible. "It was like trespassing into a forbidden area of themselves, but also it was having a reference to a film they made 30 years ago," said Guillaume, "so there's this kind of play between those things. You can imagine that they did have a son – and Gerard did have a son who did die, so there's this whole shadow of reality throughout." The director also said he first wrote it as a reaction to the death of his father, and then changed it to be about a man losing a son, a Freudian reversal if you will and a way to help Guillaume to cope.

Though a two hander, Guilaume's film features a third, more mysterious element, that of the spiritual, never fully explained, which seems vital as the story comes from the pen of a self confessed atheist. While most of the film is grounded, rooted as it is in two down to earth, straight forward tour de forces of subtlety and reserve, there is some ambiguity in the more ghostly element. When it says in the letter that they will receive a visit from their son, we do not take it too seriously. Though the desert and the vibe of the atmosphere invites the enigmatic, the tone is never sensationalised. So when Huppert's character insists her son grabbed her ankles in bed, and when Depardieu, at the film's climax, has his own marks on his skin, it comes as a genuine surprise without feeling heightened or phony. Nothing is laid out in obvious terms, nor do the characters accept or even explore their own spiritual beliefs. It is taken at face value, a pair of unexplained and perhaps unexplainable incidents. The location, as the director himself said, "creates an emotional response in everybody, if you stay longer than two days." Does the desert, its impossible heat, and the tired delirium of Isabelle and Gerard, invent the spiritual moment? Gerard himself singles out Death Valley in his marvellous book Innocent as one of the most awe inspiring places he has been to. Can environment, when coupled with deep emotion and loss, bring forth the unfathomable?

The vastness of their surroundings, the horrid heat of the sun, the impossibility of doing anything at all but sit in the shade intensifies the situation and puts more focus on the relationship between the two divorcees. They have both moved on, she going through her second divorce, he seemingly as happy as he can be. Both have reputations and are recognised by the odd American tourist, though Gerard does wind up one so called admirer who doesn't even know his name by signing his autograph "Bob De Niro".

Though not unexpectedly, Huppert and Depardieu are wonderful in their parts, playing on their own images but also creating two totally new characters. Though it's irresistible to draw parallels to the two young lovers seen in Loulou, the film has nothing in common with Valley of Love. Depardieu, now larger than he once was, stumbles and sweats in the heat, often shirtless, exhausted with the temperature and equally frustrated by the situation and itching to get back home. Isabelle, more laid back, is clearly at a cross roads. When they first meet in the hotel, he points out his weight gain. "Whatever makes you happy," she says with little care. "How can I be happy like this?" Depardieu replies. There is some self reflection going on here, but more than likely, as Huppert herself has noted in interviews, these are just roles they are playing in a film; and they just happen to be playing veteran actors who share their own first names.

For Depardieu, this was a touchy if not uncomfortable subject, given the death of his own son. Indeed, his character seems haunted, and the bridge to reality seems to be half crossed at times. "Gerard had a very particular reaction, because the film was forcing him to go back into a drama that he'd already lived," Nicloux explained. "And he's got quite a particular relationship with death, so he's not afraid of it, but the

167

suffering. Death is inevitable, we're all going to die, but it's the suffering that's difficult to accept. We can escape suffering, we can try and master that, but you can't master death."

Speaking upon the film's release in 2015, Depardieu spoke of working with Huppert again: "She was the same. Loulou was a wonderful film. Now, 35 years later, Gui has got us together again. The only difference is Isabelle is a bit more fragile than back then, but she's also more of a warrior than she was. She is the essence of woman, courageous and talented. The amazing thing was the backdrop, the heat, which is so invasive... But it's great to be back with Isabelle. This tiny woman that you can protect, but she doesn't need protecting because she can slip through your hands."

Huppert herself said that while they stayed in touch after Loulou, the chance to act together again just never came up, which is odd in itself given the amount of French films they both went on to appear in. Their natural chemistry, their brilliance together, also makes you regret they didn't have at least ten more collaborations. But then, the rarity of this team makes films like Loulou and Valley of Love all the more precious.

Valley of Love was nominated for the Palme d'Or at Cannes and both Depardieu and Huppert received nominations at the Cesar Awards (Huppert holds the record for most nominations for any actress), while reviews were largely complimentary. Screen Daily singled out Gerard's performance, writing, "Depardieu seems especially vulnerable in this film, his hulking frame is frequently half-naked and covered in perspiration as he wheezes his way through the Death Valley heat and the emotional turmoil. The more mystical, spiritual elements of the story may be hard to swallow for some but the white heat, widescreen vistas of the Death Valley locations are extremely beautiful and Depardieu and Huppert are a captivating screen couple."

Peter Bradshaw, a Depardieu admirer, was not won over by the film but found Gerard's work notable: "But Dépardieu is good: a calmer, more reflective, less egomaniacal performance than anything recently, and there is something almost heartbreakingly absurd in his whale-like obesity and that plump, cartoony face peeking out from under a cap he has bought in a local convenience store."

Anyone expecting fireworks, revelations or detailed explanations will be disappointed. Valley of Love is not that kind of film. It features two mature people dealing with loss in a beautiful but brutal landscape of extreme heat, unconvinced that anything revelatory will happen but surprised when it eventually seems to do. A beautiful, wistful film, the kind of which is sadly a rare treat these days.

Depardieu in 2016

MARSEILLE (2016-2018)

In 2015, Netflix green-lit their first French production, Marseille, the first series of which was put out in 2016, followed by a second, the final season, in 2018. Gerard Depardieu, still France's best known actor, signed up for the role of Robert Taro, the mayor of Marseille who, nearing the end of his term, supports the erection of a waterside casino which other politicians find controversial. His young deputy, importantly, opposes the decision. Meanwhile Taro becomes reluctant to run for office due to his dip in popularity and a health problem he is keeping secret from those around him.

When the series first went out, it received serious negative criticism from French reviewers, who dubbed it such charming descriptions as cow shit, an industrial accident and "cartoonish" with "ridiculous dialogue". It was hardly praised in the UK or the US either, with the New York Times writing, "Marseille had the raw material to work with. Mr. Depardieu, with his lumbering frame and bear-browed intensity, is built to be a Tony Soprano-style antihero. Marseille becomes loopier and more ridiculous as it goes."

On that note, Depardieu gives a towering performance, not quite as terrifyingly raw as the one in Welcome to New York, but a brave effort in its own right. From his first appearance, snorting coke before heading out to a packed football arena, declaring "I fucking love this city", he dominates the screen whenever he appears; and when he's off screen, it has to be said, we are waiting for him to reappear. Dan Franck, the series' creator, wrote the part with Gerard in mind, adding "Depardieu has the body to embody the character." Unlike the rotten-to-the-core sexist pig he played in Welcome to New York, Depardieu's Taro is at least a man who cares about his city. Francke explained: "We present him as a bad guy at the start, sniffing coke. But you see after that he's the opposite. He's not the cliché of the corrupt politician – he fights for the city, he's in love with the city, more than with his family."

In one of the best write ups for the show in the UK, the late Clive James revealed his fondness for Depardieu as some force of nature. "He fills the screen. Where once he filled the big screen, he now fills the small screen, so looks more screen-filling than ever. As Marseille's mayor, he has doubled in size so that the shoulders of his suit leave the screen on their way to the next banlieue. His nose, as always, looks like two lorries parked side by side, but now the lorries are the size of trains. I wouldn't call him light on his feet, but he moves smoothly, like a cargo of gravel being delivered from a camion. He dominates the screen merely by leaving no room on it for anybody else. I have always wanted to be him."

Without being biased, or at least attempting to be so, Depardieu is the main reason to watch Marseille. Without him it would have been much less effective; not because there is anything wrong with the script, acting or pacing (all are good in my view), but because Gerard is simply so convincing as Taro. Like the mayor he is playing, it's clear Depardieu has hung on to his integrity.

References

Books;
Innocent, by Gerard Depardieu
Depardieu: The Biography, by Paul Chutkow

Magazines and websites;
New York Times
Roger Ebert's website
The Guardian
Empire Magazine
Girl.com
Variety
LA Times
French Films website
Cineuropa
New Yorker
Film Comment
Decanter
Worldcrunch website
Gerald Peary's website
SBS video archive

ABOUT CHRIS WADE

Chris Wade is a UK based writer, filmmaker and musician. As well as running the acclaimed music project Dodson and Fogg, he has written books on Malcolm McDowell, Marcello Mastroianni, Robert De Niro and many others. He has also released audiobooks of his comedic fiction, such as Cutey and the Sofaguard, narrated by Rik Mayall. His other projects include Hound Dawg Magazine, for which he has interviewed such people as Sharon Stone, Donovan and Jethro Tull's Ian Anderson, and Burnt Frowner, an outlet for his poetry and art, which has included interviews with people like Roger McGough. His art films include The Apple Picker (winning Best Film at the Sydney World Film Festival, and featuring Toyah Willcox and Nigel Planer), and he's made documentaries on George Melly, Lindsay Anderson, Charlie Chaplin and Orson Welles.

More info at his website: wisdomtwinsbooks.weebly.com

Printed in the USA
CPSIA information can be obtained
at www.ICGtesting.com
LVHW020435050923
757108LV00004B/220